The Process Approach Audit Checklist for Manufacturing

Also available from ASQ Quality Press:

Process Driven Comprehensive Auditing: A New Way to Conduct ISO 9001:2000 Internal Audits
Paul C. Palmes

The Process-Focused Organization: A Transition Strategy for Success
Robert A. Gardner

The Process Auditing Techniques Guide
J. P. Russell

The Internal Auditing Pocket Guide
J. P. Russell

How to Audit the Process-Based QMS
Dennis R. Arter, Charles A. Cianfrani, and John E. (Jack) West

ISO Lesson Guide 2000: Pocket Guide to Q9001:2000, 2nd Edition
Dennis R. Arter and J. P. Russell.

Quality Audit Handbook, 2nd Edition
ASQ Quality Audit Division

Quality Audits for Improved Performance, 3rd Edition
Dennis R. Arter

The ISO 9001:2000 Auditor's Companion
Kent A. Keeney

To request a complimentary catalog of ASQ Quality Press publications, call 800-248-1946, or visit our Web site at http://qualitypress.asq.org.

The Process Approach Audit Checklist for Manufacturing

Karen Welch

ASQ Quality Press
Milwaukee, Wisconsin

American Society for Quality, Quality Press, Milwaukee 53203
© 2005 by American Society for Quality
All rights reserved. Published 2004
Printed in the United States of America

12 11 10 09 08 07   5 4 3 2

Library of Congress Cataloging-in-Publication Data

Welch, Karen, 1961–
   The process approach audit checklist for manufacturing / Karen Welch.
      p. cm.
   Includes bibliographical references and index.
   ISBN 0-87389-644-0 (alk. paper)
   1. Quality control—Auditing.   2. ISO 9000 Series Standards.   3. Process
control.   I. Title.

   TS156.W45 2004
   658.5'62—dc22   2004022390
   ISBN 0-87389-644-0

Publisher: William A. Tony
Acquisitions Editor: Annemieke Hytinen
Project Editor: Paul O'Mara
Production Administrator: Randall Benson

ASQ Mission: The American Society for Quality advances individual,
organizational, and community excellence worldwide through learning, quality
improvement, and knowledge exchange.

Attention Bookstores, Wholesalers, Schools, and Corporations: ASQ Quality Press
books, videotapes, audiotapes, and software are available at quantity discounts
with bulk purchases for business, educational, or instructional use. For
information, please contact ASQ Quality Press at 800-248-1946, or write to ASQ
Quality Press, P.O. Box 3005, Milwaukee, WI 53201-3005.

Quality Press
600 N. Plankinton Avenue
Milwaukee, Wisconsin 53203
Call toll free 800-248-1946
Fax 414-272-1734
www.asq.org
http://qualitypress.asq.org
http://standardsgroup.asq.org
E-mail: authors@asq.org

AMERICAN SOCIETY
FOR QUALITY™

To place orders or to request a free copy
of the ASQ Quality Press Publications
Catalog, including ASQ membership
information, call 800-248-1946. Visit our
Web site at www.asq.org or
http://qualitypress.asq.org.

♾ Printed on acid-free paper

Contents

TABLES OF TYPICAL AUDIT REQUIREMENTS

Preface

Finally, a comprehensive process audit checklist has been developed to be used with ISO 9001:2000! This manual was designed to assist anyone involved with conducting or planning quality system audits—including quality auditors, quality managers, quality system coordinators, management representatives, and quality engineers. In addition, potential auditees in any function or position should find the questions useful in preparing for an audit. Although the checklist could be amended to work for a service company, the manual was created with a focus on the manufacturing sector to cover common processes such as production, management, customer-related, design and development, training, purchasing, and so forth. The manual includes:

- A brief overview of the process approach

- A discussion of problem areas often found by third-party auditors

- The process audit checklist, shown in scaled-down size in the book's pages and included in full-page size on the accompanying CD-ROM as Microsoft Word files

- Forms to be used in conjunction with the process audit checklist to increase audit effectiveness, which are also included on the accompanying CD-ROM

As a third-party auditor, I have seen genuine limitations in internal quality audit processes due to inexperienced internal auditors. Many of them tell me they just aren't sure what questions to ask. After all, most of them only audit once or twice a year. How could they be as effective as someone who audits professionally? Utilizing the checklist in this manual takes the guesswork out of the internal audit process. You get many benefits, including:

1. Questions written by a third-party professional auditor.

2. The tools needed to conduct a successful audit from start to finish utilizing a true process approach. By using the checklist and its appendixes, your internal auditors will be required to audit by process and perform follow-up in associated areas to maximize benefits.

3. An audit that prepares all levels and functions in the organization for a successful third-party process audit. I continually find that people are surprised when I ask questions such as: How do you measure your processes? The main reason for this surprise is lack of training and understanding; they weren't expecting to be asked for evidence of continual improvement in their processes, especially the support processes. However, if your internal auditors ask questions like these, your management and staff will not be caught off guard during external audits.

4. The benefits of a process-based audit without hiring a professional.

Acknowledgments

First and foremost, I'd like to thank my wonderful husband, Peter M. Malmquist. Without his love and encouragement over the years, this work would not have been possible.

Special thanks to Barbara and Lex Welch for always believing in me.

I give my sincere gratitude and appreciation to Chuck Russo, Dave Dudley, and all the fine folks at ABS Quality Evaluations for allowing me the opportunity to work with some of the best in the quality field. In addition, to every ABS QE client who has endured one of my audits, I thank you. I have learned from each and every one of you.

Introduction

The goal of this manual was to produce an ISO 9001:2000 checklist that could be used to conduct a process-based audit. This checklist, presented in Chapter 3, is meant to be used as a tool by trained auditors. While it was the author's intent to cover the basic requirements of the ANSI/ISO/ASQ Q9001-2000 Standard, your organization may find the need to add questions to ensure that all requirements are addressed for your quality system. In addition, unique questions from your organization's procedures and work instructions should be added to optimize your audit. Also, I encourage you to review the forms illustrated as appendixes following Chapter 3. You may find that these forms are the most beneficial of the entire manual.

In addition to the checklist, this manual provides an overview of the process approach. It is not the author's intent to provide in-depth instruction on the process approach. Because there are many other references readily available that already thoroughly cover the subject, Chapter 1 is meant to briefly summarize the method rather than repeat information available elsewhere. This chapter also includes strategies for conducting internal audits.

Chapter 2 describes common mistakes found during third-party ISO 9001:2000 audits. By being aware of these common mistakes, your organization may be able to avoid them.

1

The Process Approach: An Overview

W hat are your key processes? What processes exist to support them? What metrics do you use to measure these processes? These are the fundamental questions that should be addressed to develop a process-based quality management system. It should not be difficult, and your system should be based on the way your company naturally does business (at least in the beginning). When you are defining your processes and their metrics, take advantage of the opportunity to optimize your overall system.

First, let's think about your key processes. Although each organization is different and must define its own unique processes, typically these processes would include:

1. Customer-related—receipt of customer requirements, contract review, order entry, and so forth

2. Design (if you perform design or any part of it)

3. Purchasing, including receipt of materials

4. Production, including maintenance, inspection, and calibration

Once these key processes have been determined, you must determine their sequence and interaction. Although a flowchart is not mandatory, it typically is the best, easiest method to use. Thus, I recommend the development of an overall process flowchart indicating how the system flows. For best results, this top-level process flowchart should be developed by a cross-functional team that includes upper-level management. For each process, determine its inputs and outputs. Use arrows to indicate direction, clearly showing what step comes next. Also, don't forget to determine measures for each process. And for each measure, establish a goal that is achievable within the next year. Many times it is also helpful to determine long-term stretch goals as well.

Then, determine your support processes. Examples include:

1. Management review

2. Internal quality audits

3. Corrective and preventive action

4. Training

5. Document control

Add these processes to your flowchart in a manner to show how they support the key processes. Also, it is important to include measures for each of these support processes as well.

Once this is accomplished, I strongly encourage you to take each key process and break it down further. Use cross-functional teams to develop an individual flowchart for each key process. Although not required by the standard, flowcharts are extremely useful tools to assist with process optimization. By clearly indicating the interactions required by different departments in the organization, the flowcharts can help identify and break down barriers that exist. We tend to operate with tunnel vision and focus on goals that optimize individual processes. Instead, we should work to optimize the process as a whole.

Why so much focus on metrics in the new standard? They are critical to your success. For one thing, you must have measures to determine how well you are performing. Are you moving in the direction of your goals? Perhaps specific action plans will help ensure that your goals are reached. If you make changes to the system, will these changes be successful in helping you reach your goals? If not, should you be focusing your time and resources on these changes? Also consider that employees will focus on what they are being measured by and/or what the organization is monitoring. Thus it is critical for your company to establish the appropriate metrics. Otherwise, your people may be working on the wrong thing.

Now that you've defined your system and its processes, you must determine how to perform an effective process-based audit. It's very important to realize that each organization is unique, and effective audit techniques vary widely by organization and individual auditor. However, I'd like to share some basic strategies with you that I have found effective across different industries. The strategies listed below are discussed in subsequent sections of this chapter:

Section 1.1   Audit by Process

Section 1.2   Interview All Functions and Levels

Section 1.3   Encourage Top Management Involvement

Section 1.4   Welcome Nonconformities as Opportunities

Section 1.5   Focus on Known Weaknesses

Section 1.6   Thoroughly Train Your Auditors

Section 1.7   Allow Time for Auditors to Adequately Prepare

Section 1.8   Encourage Auditors to Put Auditees at Ease

Section 1.9   Use a Process-Based Audit Checklist

SECTION 1.1   AUDIT BY PROCESS

Without a doubt, auditing by process is a logical approach. However, it is not always easily done by new auditors or by auditors accustomed to auditing by element. It takes more knowledge of the overall system plus improved communication skills between audit team members.

A Lead Auditor should be assigned to coordinate the audit and develop the audit plan. The audit plan should identify the processes to be audited, as well as the dates, times, auditors, and other details. Be certain to allocate time for the audit team members to meet and discuss their status. Process audits rely on strong communication among auditors to ensure that process linkages are adequately addressed.

To audit by process, each requirement in the standard that applies to that process should be covered. It is no longer as simple as auditing one section, as was done with the 1994 standard. Each auditor must understand the entire standard and must be familiar with the sections that apply to each process. Sections of the standard typically covered for each key process are:

4.2.3   Control of Documents

4.2.4   Control of Records

5.1.a   Management Commitment

5.3.d   Quality Policy

5.4.1   Quality Objectives

5.4.2   Quality Management System Planning

5.5.1   Responsibility and Authority

5.5.3   Internal Communication

6.1   Provision of Resources

6.2   Human Resources

6.3   Infrastructure

6.4   Work Environment

7.1   Planning of Product Realization

8.2.3   Monitoring and Measurement of Processes

8.5.1   Continual Improvement

8.5.2   Corrective Action

8.5.3   Preventive Action

Tables 1–4 illustrate typical sections of the standard covered for key processes including those listed above. Keep in mind that your organization may need to add or subtract from these lists.

Table 5 illustrates typical sections that should be covered for the system overall and management. Again, your organization should review the list to determine whether or not it fits your needs. An auditor should be assigned to review the overall system including its quality manual. Also, while documents and records should be sampled within each key and support process, the overall process for document and record control should also be observed. Similarly, the corrective and preventive action systems should be reviewed overall as a process, as well as within each key and support process. Furthermore, the company's internal audit process should be reviewed overall. The top management in the company should be audited for management responsibility and other areas noted in Table 5.

Please note that training requirements may be covered in each department and/or in the Human Resources department. The auditor must first determine area of responsibility as well as location of records. It is important to recognize that responsibilities may be shared by the individual departments and Human Resources. Either way, training should be recognized as a support process with its own process measure(s).

Prior to the audit of each process, the auditor should become familiar with the process flowchart and understand how the process to be audited links with other processes in the organization. Throughout the planning phase and the actual audit, the auditor should exchange information with auditors working on other processes that link to the auditor's process. For example, Auditor A is reviewing Production and Auditor B is reviewing Purchasing/Receiving. Auditor A finds a production work instruction stating that all raw materials coming into the production area must be prelabeled for traceability by the receiving warehouse. Auditor A should verify this with Auditor B to ensure that it is in agreement with Purchasing/Receiving work instructions and actual practice.

Table 1   Customer-Related Process, Typical Audit Requirements

Consult the following sections of the ANSI/ISO/ASQ Q9001-2000 Standard.

4.2.3	Control of Documents
4.2.4	Control of Records
5.1.a	Management Commitment
5.3.d	Quality Policy
5.4.1	Quality Objectives
5.4.2	Quality Management System Planning
5.5.1	Responsibility and Authority
5.5.3	Internal Communication
6.1	Provision of Resources
6.2	Human Resources
6.3	Infrastructure
6.4	Work Environment
7.1	Planning of Product Realization
7.2	Customer-Related Process
7.5.4	Customer Property
8.2.1	Customer Satisfaction
8.2.3	Monitoring and Measurement of Processes
8.4.a	Analysis of Data–Customer Satisfaction
8.5.1	Continual Improvement
8.5.2	Corrective Action
8.5.3	Preventive Action

Table 2   Design Process, Typical Audit Requirements.

Consult the following sections of the ANSI/ISO/ASQ Q9001-2000 Standard.

4.2.3	Control of Documents
4.2.4	Control of Records
5.1.a	Management Commitment
5.3.d	Quality Policy
5.4.1	Quality Objectives
5.4.2	Quality Management System Planning
5.5.1	Responsibility and Authority
5.5.3	Internal Communication
6.1	Provision of Resources
6.2	Human Resources
6.3	Infrastructure
6.4	Work Environment

Table 2   Design Process, Typical Audit Requirements. *(continued)*

7.1	Planning of Product Realization
7.3	Design and Development
7.6	Control of Monitoring and Measuring Devices (if applicable)
8.2.3	Monitoring and Measurement of Processes
8.5.1	Continual Improvement
8.5.2	Corrective Action
8.5.3	Preventive Action

Table 3   Purchasing Process, Typical Audit Requirements

Consult the following sections of the ANSI/ISO/ASQ Q9001-2000 Standard.

4.1	General Requirements–Outsourced Processes
4.2.3	Control of Documents
4.2.4	Control of Records
5.1.a	Management Commitment
5.3.d	Quality Policy
5.4.1	Quality Objectives
5.4.2	Quality Management System Planning
5.5.1	Responsibility and Authority
5.5.3	Internal Communication
6.1	Provision of Resources
6.2	Human Resources
6.3	Infrastructure
6.4	Work Environment
7.1	Planning of Product Realization
7.4	Purchasing
7.5.3	Identification and Traceability
7.5.4	Customer Property (if Purchasing assists with responsibility)
7.5.5	Preservation of Product
7.6	Control of Monitoring and Measuring Devices
8.2.4	Monitoring and Measurement of Product
8.2.3	Monitoring and Measurement of Processes
8.3	Control of Nonconforming Product
8.4.d	Analysis of Data (suppliers)
8.5.1	Continual Improvement
8.5.2	Corrective Action
8.5.3	Preventive Action

Table 4 Production Process, Typical Audit Requirements

Consult the following sections of the ANSI/ISO/ASQ Q9001-2000 Standard.

4.2.3	Control of Documents
4.2.4	Control of Records
5.1.a	Management Commitment
5.3.d	Quality Policy
5.4.1	Quality Objectives
5.4.2	Quality Management System Planning
5.5.1	Responsibility and Authority
5.5.3	Internal Communication
6.1	Provision of Resources
6.2	Human Resources
6.3	Infrastructure
6.4	Work Environment
7.1	Planning of Product Realization
7.5	Production and Service Provision
7.6	Control of Monitoring and Measuring Devices
8.2.3	Monitoring and Measurement of Processes
8.2.4	Monitoring and Measurement of Product
8.3	Control of Nonconforming Product
8.4.b	Analysis of Data (conformity to product requirements)
8.5.1	Continual Improvement
8.5.2	Corrective Action
8.5.3	Preventive Action

Table 5 Management Process, Typical Audit Requirements

Consult the following sections of the ANSI/ISO/ASQ Q9001-2000 Standard.

4	Quality Management System
5	Management Responsibility
6	Resource Management
7.1	Planning of Product Realization
8.1	Measurement, Analysis, and Improvement: General
8.2	Monitoring and Measurement
8.4	Analysis of Data
8.5	Improvement

SECTION 1.2   INTERVIEW ALL FUNCTIONS AND LEVELS

It is important to interview all functions and levels during internal audits. This is what I commonly refer to as "spreading the joy." In other words, let everyone experience the audit process. Of course, unless you have a small organization, time does not permit everyone being interviewed at each audit. However, you should include as many individuals as possible. Be certain to include persons in each department and at all levels, including the site manager, department managers, supervisors, and operators. Your organization should have auditors who feel comfortable interviewing operators as well as top management.

Beware of areas where only one person has all the answers. For example, if the department manager developed the ISO system for his area, be wary if he tries to dissuade you from talking to others who work for him. It is important that everyone understand their role in the system. Granted, a supervisor or operator may not have the answer to a question that the department is responsible for. Nor would they be expected to. However, they should be knowledgeable of their area of responsibility in the process. Thus, it is important for the auditor to cover all levels.

SECTION 1.3   ENCOURAGE TOP MANAGEMENT INVOLVEMENT

To optimize the audit process, top management should be involved and should consider the audit a priority. Typically, all it takes is for the top manager to ask questions of his staff to obtain their participation. The auditor should not have to plead with personnel to set up the audit. Although the person developing the audit schedule should be flexible in working with the department managers, scheduling of the audit should be considered a priority by the department managers.

Of course, top management involvement should apply to the entire quality system, not just the audit process. Without their buy-in and commitment, the system will not be optimized.

SECTION 1.4   WELCOME NONCONFORMITIES AS OPPORTUNITIES

It is critical for the organization to welcome nonconformities as opportunities. Nonconformities that are found during the audit should be viewed as quality system issues rather than personnel issues. Something in the system was not working properly, and the system must be corrected. If nonconformities are viewed as negative or if personnel are punished, it will be difficult to optimize the quality system. Personnel will not voluntarily offer information if they are fearful. However, if the organization views the audit as a means to improve the system, personnel will be much more likely to elaborate on questions that are asked of them.

The philosophy of the organization starts at the top; thus, top management must be involved, as noted in Section 1.3.

SECTION 1.5   FOCUS ON KNOWN WEAKNESSES

As we all know, the audit is based on sampling. With adequate preparation, the auditor should be able to greatly improve the benefit of the audit by focusing on the most appropriate areas. The auditor should study the company's metrics, and during the audit should focus on areas with known weaknesses. For example, if trend charts indicate that one particular production area is creating the majority of the scrap, the auditor should focus on that area. Yes, other areas should be sampled as well. In fact, it is best to audit each and every production area. However, by spending more time on areas creating the most internal scrap and customer complaints, the auditor is best serving the organization.

SECTION 1.6   THOROUGHLY TRAIN YOUR AUDITORS

To optimize the audit process, every auditor should initially have formal training on the current standard as well as auditing techniques. Also, when possible, it is best for a new auditor to witness other audits prior to becoming qualified to audit alone. It is not fair to the organization or the individual when adequate training does not occur. The organization loses because the audit process is not optimized. The individual loses by being put in a position that he or she is not ready for, and few people are comfortable in this situation.

The process audit checklist illustrated in Chapter 3 is an excellent tool to assist a new auditor. However, it merely defines questions for the auditor—it does not tell the auditor what to do with the response. Thus, even with the checklist, training is critical for a successful audit. Ongoing, periodic refresher training for all auditors should be considered.

SECTION 1.7   ALLOW TIME FOR
AUDITORS TO ADEQUATELY PREPARE

Many audits are not optimized because the auditors are not given adequate time to prepare. Thus, when auditors are assigned, it is important to build auditor prep time into the schedule. This allows the auditor's management to see how much time will be required. It is not enough to dedicate personnel's time for the audit only, without considering preparation.

Because auditors may not audit their own work, many times they will be auditing in areas they are not familiar with. Preparation time is critical for the auditor to study documentation, trends in metrics, potential weak areas, and so forth. It may be helpful for the auditor to prepare for the audit away from his or her normal workstation to avoid distraction.

SECTION 1.8   ENCOURAGE AUDITORS
TO PUT AUDITEES AT EASE

To optimize the audit process, the auditor should try to put the auditee at ease. A nervous auditee sometimes makes mistakes and normally does not openly communicate. On the other hand, if the auditee is relaxed, in most cases the auditor will be able to obtain much more information. For instance, sometimes, if I suspect that an auditee is nervous, I will look for photographs of pets at his or her workstation. Then, asking about the pet normally makes the auditee light up. (I choose pets because that is what I can relate to, but children work just as well.) When an auditee realizes we have something in common, he or she tends to relax. Of course, the auditor must always remain in control and stay on track, but taking 30 seconds to ask what an auditee thought about the game last night will normally be worthwhile and beneficial to the audit.

SECTION 1.9   USE A
PROCESS-BASED AUDIT CHECKLIST

Most auditors do not audit on a regular basis. In fact, many of them only audit a couple of days out of the year. It is often difficult for these auditors to determine the appropriate questions to ask. And although the process-based audit is much more beneficial to the organization, new auditors or those who seldom audit sometimes find it more complex. Thus, the use of a process-based audit checklist is highly recommended. The checklist in Chapter 3 is one example to consider. Use it as a starting point, adding your own questions pertaining to your organization's unique procedures and work instructions.

2

Common ISO 9001:2000 Mistakes to Avoid

C ommon mistakes found during ISO 9001:2000 audits are listed below and discussed in subsequent sections:

SECTION 2.1   IMPROPER EXCLUSIONS IDENTIFIED

Often companies identify improper exclusions. Only requirements in section 7 (Product Realization) may be excluded from your quality system. You may exclude only requirements that you do not perform, and you must include justification in your quality manual.

The problem with exclusions normally lies with design and development. Organizations tend to automatically assume that if they were certified to ISO 9002:1994, they may exclude design. That is not always the case. They may have chosen to pursue only ISO 9002:1994 (as opposed to ISO 9001:1994) even though they performed design. With the new standard, you may not exclude design if you do it. And in addition, if you perform any part of design, you may exclude only those requirements that you do not perform. For example, an organization may not perform any part of design except validation. If that is the case, it may exclude all of section 7.3, except 7.3.6 (Design and Development Validation). Another common design-related problem that third-party auditors encounter involves outsourced design processes. These may not be excluded and must be controlled by the organization (see Section 2.5 later in this chapter).

Another problem found during ISO 9001:2000 audits is failure of the organization to justify the exclusions in the quality manual. You must document the justifications in the quality manual.

SECTION 2.2   FAILURE TO ADEQUATELY DEFINE EACH PROCESS

As explained in Chapter 1, each process must be identified and defined. These processes should include not only your manufacturing processes, but their support processes as well. Typically, companies do rather well identifying their production, design, purchasing, and customer-related processes. The failure normally occurs with support processes such as training, internal quality audit, corrective and preventive action, and management review. These processes must be included.

SECTION 2.3   FAILURE TO ADEQUATELY DETERMINE SEQUENCE AND INTERACTION

After the processes are identified, the organization often fails to take the next step. The sequence and interaction of the identified processes must be defined. In other words, in what order do the processes occur? How do the processes work together? Typically, the simplest method to use is a process map that makes it easy to show the steps that occur and how they interact. For example: What comes first, an order or production? In an order-driven system, the order comes first. Prior to production, other processes such as purchasing occur. A process map clearly illustrates this sequence of events. Most processes do not stand alone; they interact with other processes. For example, the Purchasing department must know what has been ordered by the customer and/or scheduled by Production prior to ordering material from a supplier. As noted in Chapter 2, you should fully understand the interactions between the processes and work toward optimization of the system as a whole rather than optimization of each individual process.

SECTION 2.4   FAILURE TO IDENTIFY MEASURES FOR EACH PROCESS

The standard clearly requires that the organization must monitor, measure, and analyze each of its processes. It often seems that organizations begin the audit process assuming they have identified their measures when they actually have not. Or, more often, they actually have these metrics but do not realize they have them.

First, let's talk about organizations that assume they have the measures they need. In general, organizations do very well with measures for manufacturing, because most companies have always done this. Metrics for the customer-related, purchasing, and design processes, on the other hand, are often available but are usually somewhat weaker and not as well defined. Typically, the support processes create the problems, because these metrics are usually more difficult to define. And many organizations make the mistake of overlooking the measures for these processes. Examples of support processes often overlooked would include training, internal quality audit, corrective action, and preventive action processes. Some examples of applicable measures for these support processes are:

- *Training:* Pretest score/posttest score; percentage of employees completing annual training plans

- *Internal quality audit:* Number of process audits completed on schedule; number of nonconformities issued (keep in mind that a higher number may not be bad); number of trained auditors

- *Corrective action:* Number of customer complaints; number of corrective actions past due

Secondly, let's talk about organizations that do not realize they have the necessary metrics. Occasionally when I go into an audit and ask for the metrics for each process, the organization stumbles and cannot identify them. More often than not—usually due to lack of training and/or lack of understanding—they actually have these metrics but are unaware of it. (Of course as an auditor, I cannot give them the answer even though I see it right in front of me.) Be certain the leadership team has a strong understanding of process measures. They should understand their process measures better than their auditor, not the other way around!

I believe that the focus on measures is a great benefit in the ANSI/ISO/ASQ Q9001-2000 Standard. Measures, if done correctly, drive the organization to meet common goals. On the other hand, if done haphazardly, they can be dangerous. People typically will focus their efforts to improve what the organization is monitoring. Thus, if the organization determines the wrong metrics, their personnel will be headed in the wrong direction!

Ensure that the organization has a metric for each process identified, including support processes. Be safe. Why not include a column in your process matrix for measures? And be smart. The leadership should spend time and take care to develop the appropriate metrics to drive the organization in the right direction.

SECTION 2.5   FAILURE TO IDENTIFY CONTROL OF OUTSOURCED PROCESSES

According to ISO N526R, the term *outsource* is interchangeable with *subcontract.*[1] When the organization outsources a process that impacts product conformity, that process must be controlled. Such processes would include product design and development as well as manufacturing. Thus, if you outsource these processes, you may not exclude them, and you must identify how you control them. Typically, this control would be through requirements addressed by the standard in purchasing.

It is a common mistake for an organization to omit the control of these subcontracted processes from its quality system. The system must include these processes in its scope, and the methods to manage and control these processes should be clearly defined. The organization should treat the suppliers of these processes the same as it treats its other suppliers. All suppliers should go through a selection and evaluation process, and periodic reevaluation should occur.

SECTION 2.6   FAILURE TO INCLUDE "LEGIBLE" IN PROCEDURE FOR DOCUMENTS

Although minor compared to other issues discussed, almost every document review I have conducted for ISO 9001:2000 has excluded legibility of documents. This occurs primarily because we are used to discussing legibility of records per ISO 1994—but legibility of documents is also now a requirement. It expands the concept to include all documents, not just records. Because a record is a special type of document, if an organization's documented procedures cover only records, this would not be adequate to meet the requirement. For example, if your organization allows personnel to handwrite changes or additions to procedures, it is logical that these handwritten changes and additions must be legible. Unfortunately, this is not always the case, as I can attest. Thus, the need to require legibility of documents is apparent. Although this requirement may seem obvious to the organization, it must be documented.

SECTION 2.7   QUALITY OBJECTIVES NOT ESTABLISHED AT RELEVANT FUNCTIONS AND LEVELS

Probably one of the weakest areas in many quality systems revolves around quality objectives. The standard tells us that they must be established at relevant functions and levels. What are "relevant" functions and levels? For optimal benefits, this would mean most functions and levels. The key to establishing meaningful objectives is to begin with those at the top level. However, the organization should not stop there. Each area should establish objectives to support the top level. Then, these objectives should be carried through to the different levels. Objectives that are meaningful to top management are not normally best for personnel in operations. Thus, it is important to state the objectives in terms that personnel can relate to. Everyone must be able to understand how they impact the objectives, as further discussed later in this chapter in Section 2.12.

Consider an organization with a quality objective to increase customer satisfaction. Each area should establish objectives to improve customer satisfaction to support the organization's goals. For example, Purchasing may establish an objective to reduce material costs to partially pass on to the customer. Maintenance may establish an objective to reduce equipment breakdown, thus improving on-time delivery to the customer. This type of idea should be used for each process.

SECTION 2.8   FAILURE TO COMMUNICATE THE EFFECTIVENESS OF THE QUALITY MANAGEMENT SYSTEM

Often companies do not do an adequate job communicating the effectiveness of the quality management system. When I ask employees how their quality system is doing, the typical answer is something like "Pretty good." When I go on to ask how they know, it is not uncommon for them to tell me that management lets them know if they do something wrong. Thus, since they have not heard anything, everything must be okay. Certainly, that does not meet the intent of the standard. It is important that the company communicate the effectiveness of the quality management system to all employees. It is recommended that this communication occur through more than one medium.

First, the management should verbally discuss the effectiveness of the system. Let the employees know how well the company is doing. Tell them how well they are meeting their quality objectives. Let them know the level of customer satisfaction. If there have been customer complaints, share them with the employees. Occasionally, companies tell me they do not want to share the information because it is too confidential. This requirement does not mean that all metrics must be shared companywide. However, measures should be developed and shared to gauge the effectiveness of the quality system without compromising confidentiality of the company. Communication with your employees is instrumental in developing a strong quality system. They need to know where they stand and what needs improvement. Sometimes a company will bring all employees together annually to share the status of the business with them. This is a strong method for communication, but annually is not enough. Consider supplementing this type of annual meeting with more frequent but less extensive meetings. Perhaps the communication of objectives could be added to meetings that already exist, such as shift change meetings, weekly department meetings, or safety meetings.

Second, it is highly recommended that the status of the objectives and other metrics be posted in various areas visible to the employees. When they are asked about the effectiveness of the quality system, they should have an answer and know what it is based on. When I am auditing and ask about the effectiveness of a system, I am encouraged when the employee takes me to charts of the metrics and explains them to me. Keep in mind that posting performance to objectives should not replace the verbal communication. Verbal communication is important to ensure that employees understand the meaning. Posting the objectives should be in support of the verbal explanation.

SECTION 2.9   INCOMPLETE MANAGEMENT REVIEW RECORDS

The standard is very specific about what is required for management review. More often than not, when auditing companies new to the standard, I issue a nonconformity against management review because the record is incomplete. It seems to be very difficult to remember to include all the requirements in the review meeting. Companies that avoid this problem normally utilize a checklist as a supplement to their meeting minutes. It is recommended that you develop a checklist that includes all management review requirements of the standard. An example is illustrated in Appendix G (Management Review Meeting Checklist) at the end of this book. It differs from Appendix E (Management Review) in that Appendix E is a checklist to be used during an internal audit, whereas Appendix G is to be used during the management review itself. During your meeting, the checklist may then be used as an agenda, with each item checked off as it is discussed. Sometimes, notes are taken directly on the checklist, but that is something to be determined by the company. If you prefer to generate separate meeting minutes, that would suffice. However, keeping one record may be easier to maintain.

SECTION 2.10   COMPETENCY NOT DEFINED

Section 3.9.12 of ANSI/ISO/ASQ Q9000:2000 defines *competence* as "demonstrated ability to apply knowledge and skills."[2] How do you determine if your employees are competent? If someone was competent to do a particular job when they were hired 20 years ago, are they still competent today? These are questions your organization should consider. Just because an employee is highly educated does not mean that the employee is competent for a certain position. The organization should determine what skills and education are needed for each position (for example, the job description). As individuals are hired, it should be determined whether they have the necessary skills and education. If a requirement is missing from the person's background, training requirements should be determined. However, this alone does not satisfy the competency requirement, which involves "demonstrated ability." Often this is satisfied through job qualification for hourly employees and performance reviews for salaried employees. Periodic performance evaluations may take care of the evaluation of ongoing competency.

The training process should be strongly linked to the achievement of continual improvement, discussed in Section 2.21. Personnel should receive ongoing training to grow and discover new ideas to improve their processes.

SECTION 2.11   FAILURE TO EVALUATE EFFECTIVENESS OF TRAINING

Evaluating the effectiveness of training is not always a simple task; thus, often it is overlooked or ignored because the organization does not know how to perform the evaluation. There are several ways to evaluate this effectiveness, ranging from simple to elaborate methods. A few of the simpler methods are discussed below.

A common approach utilizes pretests and posttests. This way, you know how much subject knowledge the employee possessed coming into the training and how much the employee gained during the training. With a little preplanning, this method is simple to initiate and meets the standard's requirements.

Another common approach is to evaluate the training obtained during the employee's performance review. Did the training help the employee to improve job performance? This method should work—although the result may have been due to multiple factors, not just the training.

Another method sometimes used is to evaluate the organization or department's overall performance. Did the training provided improve the performance? This method is the least direct, but is helpful in looking at the big picture.

I recommend utilizing a combination of all three methods listed above to get the best evaluation of training. Training is normally a costly investment and should be monitored to ensure that the organization is getting its money's worth. I worked with a very large company that required each employee to obtain a significant amount of training hours each year. Accomplishment of this task was linked to the company's bonus program; however, the subject of the training did not matter. We commended the company for enriching its employees' lives, but suggested that at least some of the training be directly linked to the job so the organization would benefit as well as the individual. Evaluating training effectiveness should be a very helpful tool for the organization to learn which training helps them improve.

SECTION 2.12   PERSONNEL NOT AWARE OF HOW THEY CONTRIBUTE TO THE ACHIEVEMENT OF THE QUALITY OBJECTIVES

Just communicating the quality objectives is not enough to meet the requirements of the standard. The organization must make certain that its employees know how they contribute to their achievement. Section 6.2.2.d of the standard is another area that gets written up quite often during an audit. Employees must understand more than just what the objectives are; they must understand how they contribute to them.

For example, if one of the organization's objectives is to improve on-time delivery, then each employee should understand his or her role. Many times, personnel outside of Production do not recognize this. For example, Customer Service representatives should understand that to improve on-time delivery, they must be certain the company is capable of meeting the customer's due date prior to taking an order.

To further illustrate, consider a company with a quality objective to reduce the number of customer complaints. Occasionally, only the coordinator of the complaint system is aware of the number of customer complaints. To meet the requirements of ISO 9001:2000, the organization normally publishes these numbers. However, many individuals outside of

Production do not understand how they impact these objectives. These individuals might be in Maintenance or Purchasing. To improve, the company should ensure that these individuals understand how they can positively impact the number of customer complaints through areas such as on-time delivery (Maintenance) and/or product quality (Purchasing).

SECTION 2.13   METHOD OF CUSTOMER COMMUNICATION NOT ESTABLISHED

It is amazing how often I ask an organization about its process to communicate with customers, and the interviewees seem surprised by my question. Perhaps they were caught unaware because this requirement is much more clearly defined in the 2000 standard than it was in the 1994 version. The standard tells us that an organization must define its process to communicate with customers regarding product information, customer feedback (including complaints), questions, and orders (including amendments). How does an organization let the customer know who to contact for these issues? Often, this is handled either by Sales or Customer Service.

Another possible reason for not having an established method of communicating with customers is because manufacturing plants sometimes assume this function is being covered by the corporate office. If this is the case, the process should be defined so that each location is aware of what is done. If the office that handles customer communication is not part of the site being audited, it should be controlled as an outsourced process to ensure that requirements of the standard are being met (see Section 2.5 earlier in this chapter). Conducting an internal audit of the office would be a method of evaluation and control.

SECTION 2.14   "REEVALUATION" OF SUPPLIERS NOT PERFORMED

"Reevaluation" of suppliers is another term used in the 2000 standard that we did not see in the 1994 standard. In the past, companies would select and evaluate their suppliers initially, with little done afterward unless there was a problem. This is not acceptable with the 2000 standard. The organization must reevaluate its suppliers at some point. It is recommended that this reevaluation be done at periodic intervals to assess quality, service, and delivery. The organization should also evaluate its suppliers' responses to any corrective action requests that may have been issued. Do your suppliers create reoccurring problems for you? A summary of suppliers' performance should be included in the management review.

Suppliers are critical to today's organizations, and their assessment can lead to improvement of your products. By tracking each supplier and assessing its performance, the organization is identifying problems—and should be either forcing an underperforming supplier to improve or finding another supplier. A small investment in this area to develop the process may be very beneficial to the organization.

SECTION 2.15   "REVALIDATION" OF PROCESSES NOT PERFORMED

Another new and often overlooked requirement involves the "revalidation" of special processes. If you perform a process such as welding, where you cannot determine the result until the product is actually used, you must periodically "revalidate" the process. Thus, validating the process at start-up is no longer enough. This is a requirement that most people already perform, but often they are not ready for the question during an audit. If you have special processes, be prepared to define how you validate them as well as how you "revalidate" them. Depending upon the consequences of product failure, you should revalidate as often as needed for the process to be effective or as regulated by the government at a minimum for safety concerns.

SECTION 2.16   NO RECORD FOR CUSTOMER PROPERTY

Keeping complete and accurate records of customer property continues to be a problem during ISO 9001:2000 audits just as it was with ISO 1994 audits. Customer property involves anything that belongs to your customer that your organization controls. This may include raw material, labels, packaging, tooling, software, intellectual property, or equipment. If anything of this nature is lost, damaged, or cannot be used for some reason, it must be reported to the customer with a record maintained. It is not uncommon to find a weakness in this process. Often, the process itself is not well defined within the organization, nor is the responsibility for the record. The organization should establish who is responsible for reporting problems of this nature to the customer. In addition, the record should be established as a quality record. And if you have not yet experienced this problem, do not wait for it to happen before you establish a record. Go ahead and define your process. You may have an empty file in the beginning, but you will be ready if it should occur.

Lost or damaged customer property typically does not occur on a regular basis, thus making it a process that is often difficult to remember when it does happen. Failure to keep this record is a common nonconformity found during third-party audits. Perhaps it might be helpful to periodically review the process with the organization to ensure that it is not forgotten when needed.

SECTION 2.17   RAW MATERIAL SHELF LIFE UNKNOWN

While auditing preservation of product, I typically sample raw materials for indication of expiration date or shelf life. If any of the organization's raw materials have a shelf life, there should be a process to monitor and adhere to it. While this process is normally found in organizations that have a large number of raw materials with shelf lives, it is often overlooked in organizations that have only a handful. Be certain that your organization is aware of any raw materials that have an expiration date, and if applicable, determine your process to handle. Be cautious of certain resins, glues, paints, and so forth.

SECTION 2.18   WHEN CALIBRATED EQUIPMENT FOUND OUT OF TOLERANCE, NO RECORD OF ASSESSMENT

What happens if you have a piece of equipment calibrated, and it is found out of tolerance? The common answer I receive is that the equipment is adjusted until it comes in tolerance. Yes, this correction should be made before the instrument is used again. However, this alone does not satisfy the requirements of the standard. When an instrument is found outside of tolerance, the standard tells us that the validity of previous measurements must be assessed and recorded. In other words, you must assess the severity of the out-of-tolerance condition and determine whether it impacted product measurements. If so, you must then assess the situation to try to determine when the out-of-tolerance condition developed, possibly going back to the prior calibration. The product measured with this instrument should be evaluated to determine whether the customer received out-of-spec product. A record for this entire assessment must be defined and maintained.

SECTION 2.19   NO PROACTIVE METHOD TO DETERMINE CUSTOMER SATISFACTION

The standard clearly requires the organization to monitor customer satisfaction; however, it leaves the *what* and *how* up to the organization. Often organizations, especially smaller ones, utilize customer complaints as their measure of customer satisfaction. While this is indeed one measure, it should be coupled with a proactive approach. If done properly, a proactive approach may prevent a problem from occurring or at least may reduce its impact. The important thing is for the organization to seek out information rather than wait for a complaint.

One proactive technique is the customer survey, which may be written or verbal. If the decision is made to use a verbal survey, either formal or informal, it is important to record the results to assist with evaluation. And if you get a negative response, I strongly recommend that your organization address it with the customer in a timely manner. If you are going to ask the customer how you are doing, you should be prepared to make necessary adjustments to improve. If you do not address their concerns, customers may stop responding—or worse yet, may take their business elsewhere.

SECTION 2.20   NO EVIDENCE OF CONTINUAL IMPROVEMENT

I cannot tell you how many times I ask an organization for an example of continual improvement and they provide an example of a negative trend! Be prepared to discuss and provide examples of continual improvement in each process, including support. The continual improvement process may occur with breakthrough projects or through many small steps. Each area should be able to provide examples of projects for continual improvement as well as examples of positive trends. There is no requirement that the data be charted, but it certainly is easier for the organization to identify and prove positive trends with charts. I recommend the use of charts for data analysis. Not only does it make the audit easier, but more importantly, it helps the employees of your organization to visualize what is happening.

SECTION 2.21 LACK OF DEFINITION FOR AUDIT CRITERIA, SCOPE, AND METHODS

For internal audits, the new standard requires audit criteria, scope, frequency, and methods to be defined. Normally, frequency is not a problem, but the other areas are often not clear. ANSI/ISO/ASQ Q9000:2000 defines *audit criteria* as a "set of policies, procedures, or requirements used as a reference."[3] Thus, for your internal audit, you must define the documents to be used as a reference, such as procedures, standards, or customers' supplier quality manuals. The scope of the audit would address the extent of the audit, such as the scope on your ISO certificate. If all of the quality system is not going to be covered during this particular audit, the scope should state this fact. The methods to be used include your auditing techniques, such as document review, interview of personnel, or review of records. Be certain these items are clearly defined for each audit.

SECTION 2.22 DISREGARDING A REQUIREMENT

I have never understood why an organization simply ignores a requirement of the standard. Perhaps the hope is that the auditor will overlook the requirement or run out of time. This is a mistake for the organization. Address every requirement. It is far better to define your process and in so doing, prompt thought and discussion for your third-party auditor rather than not address an issue at all. If you simply say you do not know or you forgot, the auditor will have no choice except to issue a nonconformance. For example, rather than ignoring training effectiveness because you do not feel you fully understand it, use available resources to learn as much as you can. Even though you may not be an expert, develop some kind of process and implement it. The auditor will let you know whether it meets the intent of the standard. And at least you will have something in place for the requirement, which may possibly save you from getting a major nonconformity.

3

The Checklist

In Chapters 1 and 2, this manual presented an overview of the process approach and a list of common mistakes encountered in ISO 9001:2000 audits. Now it's time to move on to our primary topic: the process approach audit checklist, shown on the following pages in scaled-down size and included as Microsoft Word files in full-page size on the CD-ROM accompanying this book.

GUIDELINES FOR USE

The questions in the checklist were derived from the ISO 9001:2000 standard (entry 4 in the list of References). The first step is to determine how the positions indicated on the checklist coincide with positions in your organization. For example, the checklist assumes you have both a purchasing manager and a shipping manager. If your organization combines these functions into a material manager, however, the auditor would not need to ask duplicate questions under Purchasing and Shipping when interviewing the material manager. Or, if you perform design functions but do not have a specific design lab, questions designated for the design lab tech should be merged in with the regular lab tech questions.

This manual should be used as a tool and does not take the place of auditor training. The checklist assumes the auditor will know what to do with the information after the question is asked—thus it should be used only by trained auditors. The auditors may gather some information themselves and may not need to ask every question. However, they should keep in mind that it is important to know not only that the requirements are met, but also that the interviewee understands how they are met. This is especially important for those preparing for a third-party audit. Also, the appendixes at the back of this manual are critical to the success of the audit and should be self-explanatory for a trained auditor.

And most importantly, for maximum benefits, the organization must add its own specific questions pertaining to procedures and work instructions.

Section 3.1 Management Process

	Standard Clause	Function/Level	Question	Result
1	4.1.a	Plant manager	What processes do you manage and where are they identified?	
2	4.1.b	Plant manager	What is the sequence and interaction of these processes?	
3	4.1.b	Plant manager	How do your processes link with the other processes external to your plant but within your company? *(This question would only apply to a company with multiple sites.)*	
4	4.1.d 5.1.e 6.1	Plant manager	How do you ensure availability of resources and information needed to support the operation and monitoring of your processes?	

Auditor Name _____   Date of Audit _____

Section 3.1 Management Process

	Standard Clause	Function/Level	Question	Result
5	4.1.e 8.2.3	Plant manager	How do you monitor and measure your processes? Please provide examples. *(For each process defined in #1, there should be a measurement.)*	
6	4.1	Plant manager	Do you outsource any processes? If so, how do you control these processes?	
7	5.1.a	Plant manager	How do you communicate to your plant the importance of meeting customer, regulatory, and statutory requirements?	
8	5.1.c 5.4.1	Plant manager	What are the quality objectives for your plant and how were they established?	

Auditor Name _____   Date of Audit _____

Section 3.1 Management Process

	Standard Clause	Function/Level	Question	Result
9	5.2	Plant manager	How do you make sure that customer requirements are determined, and that they are met with the goal of improving customer satisfaction?	
10	5.3.e	Plant manager	The standard requires the quality policy to be reviewed for continuing suitability. How is this done? *(Auditor should see some evidence that this has occurred.)*	
11	5.3.a 5.1.b	Plant manager	How was your quality policy established? How is it appropriate to the purpose of the company?	
12	5.3.b	Plant manager	The quality policy must have a commitment to comply with requirements and include continual improvement. *(If the auditor does not find this, ask the plant manager how this requirement is met.)*	

Auditor Name _____   Date of Audit _____

Section 3.1 Management Process

	Standard Clause	Function/Level	Question	Result
13	5.3.c	Plant manager	How does the quality policy provide a structure for establishing and reviewing quality objectives?	
14	5.3.d	Plant manager	How do you ensure that the quality policy is communicated and understood?	
15	5.4.1	Plant manager	For what functions and levels have quality objectives been established?	
16	5.4.1	Plant manager	Please explain how the objectives are measurable and consistent with the policy.	

Auditor Name _____   Date of Audit _____

Section 3.1 Management Process

	Standard Clause	Function/Level	Question	Result
17	5.5.1	Plant manager	Where are responsibilities and authorities defined, and how are they communicated?	
18	5.4.2.a	Plant manager	How is the planning of the quality system carried out to meet requirements and quality objectives?	
19	5.4.2.b	Plant manager	How do you ensure that the integrity of the quality management system is maintained when changes are planned and implemented?	
20	5.6 4.2.4	Plant manager	*Sample management review records to ensure that they meet requirements of record control procedures. Use Appendix C: Records.*	
21	5.6	Plant manager	Describe your process for management review.	

Auditor Name _____   Date of Audit _____

Section 3.1 Management Process

	Standard Clause	Function/Level	Question	Result
22	5.6	Plant manager	How often do you conduct management reviews?	
23	5.6	Plant manager	May I see records of management reviews conducted since the last internal quality audit? *(Auditor to verify that records show all requirements of the standard were met. Use Appendix E: Management Review.)*	
24	5.5.2	Plant manager	Who is your management representative and how was this person appointed?	
25	5.5.2	Plant manager	What are the management rep's responsibilities?	
26	5.5.3	Plant manager	What communication processes are established within your plant?	

Auditor Name _____   Date of Audit _____

Section 3.1 Management Process

	Standard Clause	Function/Level	Question	Result
27	5.5.3	Plant manager	How do you communicate the effectiveness of your quality management system to your plant?	
28	6.2.1	Plant manager	How do you determine competence of your employees?	
29	6.2.2.d	Plant manager	How do you ensure that personnel in your plant are aware of the importance of their jobs and how they contribute to achievement of quality objectives?	
30	7.1	Plant manager	What are your processes for product realization?	

Auditor Name _____ Date of Audit _____

Section 3.1 Management Process

	Standard Clause	Function/Level	Question	Result
31	7.1	Plant manager	What is the output of your planning of product realization?	
32	8.2.3	Plant manager	What do you do when planned results are not achieved? *(Examples of correction and corrective action should be provided.)*	
33	8.5.1	Plant manager	Please provide examples of continual improvement.	

Auditor Name _____ Date of Audit _____

Section 3.1 Management Process

	Standard Clause	Function/Level	Question	Result
34	8.5.2 8.5.3	Plant manager	Have you personally participated in any corrective and/or preventive actions? If yes, please give an example.	
35	4.2.2	Quality manager	Show me how the quality manual meets requirements of the standard.	
36	6.1	Determine by observation of plant overall	Do resources appear to be adequate to maintain the quality system and continually improve its effectiveness? To enhance customer satisfaction by meeting customer requirements?	
37	6.3	Determine by observation of plant overall	Infrastructure: Does the plant include the appropriate workspace, equipment, and supporting services such as transport or communication?	
38	6.4	Determine by observation of plant overall	Is the plant's work environment appropriate to meet product requirements?	

Auditor Name _____   Date of Audit _____

Section 3.1 Management Process

Use the following section to develop your own questions:

Procedure/Work Instruction	Function/Level	Question	Result

Auditor Name _____   Date of Audit _____

Section 3.2 Customer-Related Process

	Standard Clause	Function/Level	Question	Result
1	4.1.a	Manager	What process(es) do you manage?	
2	4.1.b	Manager	How do your processes link with the other processes in the company? *(Examples might be design, scheduling, production, etc.)*	
3	5.1.a	Manager	How do you communicate to your area the importance of meeting customer, regulatory, and statutory requirements?	
4	5.3.d	Manager	How do you ensure that the quality policy is communicated and understood?	

Auditor Name _____   Date of Audit _____

Section 3.2 Customer-Related Process

	Standard Clause	Function/Level	Question	Result
5	5.4.1	Manager	What are the quality objectives for your area?	
6	5.5.1	Manager	Where are responsibilities and authorities defined, and how are they communicated?	
7	5.5.1	Manager	How are duties divided up among the customer service reps (by region, by customer, etc.)?	
8	5.5.3	Manager	What communication processes are established within your area?	
9	5.5.3	Manager	How do you communicate the effectiveness of your quality management system to your area?	

Auditor Name _____   Date of Audit _____

Section 3.2 Customer-Related Process

	Standard Clause	Function/Level	Question	Result
10	5.4.2	Manager	How do you ensure that the integrity of the quality management system is maintained when changes are planned and implemented?	
11	6.2.1	Manager	How do you determine competence of your employees?	
12	6.2.2.d	Manager	How do you ensure that personnel in your area are aware of the importance of their jobs and how they contribute to achievement of quality objectives?	
13	7.2.1.a	Manager	How do you determine requirements specified by the customer, including delivery and postdelivery requirements?	

Auditor Name _____   Date of Audit _____

Section 3.2 Customer-Related Process

	Standard Clause	Function/Level	Question	Result
14	7.2.1.b	Manager	How do you determine requirements known for intended use, even though not stated by the customer?	
15	7.2.1.c	Manager	How do you determine regulatory and statutory requirements of the product?	
16	7.2.1.d	Manager	How do you determine any other requirements?	
17	7.2.2	Manager	What is your process to review the order prior to acceptance? *(The answer should include ensuring that product requirements are defined, resolving any differences, and ensuring that the organization has the ability to meet the requirements.)*	

Auditor Name _____   Date of Audit _____

Section 3.2 Customer-Related Process

	Standard Clause	Function/Level	Question	Result
18	7.2.2	Manager	Who has the authority to review the order to ensure that all requirements can be met?	
19	7.2.2	Manager	What is your record indicating the results of the review?	
20	7.2.2	Manager	What do you do if customers do not provide documentation of their requirements? *(The answer should include a method to confirm customer requirements prior to acceptance.)*	
21	7.2.2	Manager	What happens if an order is changed? *(Ensure that documents are updated and relevant personnel are notified of change.)*	
22	7.2.3	Manager	What is your process to communicate with your customer regarding product information, contracts, customer complaints, etc.?	

Auditor Name _____   Date of Audit _____

Section 3.2 Customer-Related Process

	Standard Clause	Function/Level	Question	Result
23	7.5.4	Manager	Do you have any customer property? If so, how is it controlled? *(This could include product, software, equipment, tooling, labels, etc.)*	
24	7.5.4	Manager	What is your record for customer property that is lost, damaged, or otherwise unsuitable for use and to indicate it was reported to the customer?	
25	8.2.1	Manager	What are your customers' perceptions as to whether customer service has met their requirements? How do you know this?	
26	8.2.3/ 4.1.e	Manager	How do you monitor and measure your process? Please provide examples.	

Auditor Name _____   Date of Audit _____

Section 3.2 Customer-Related Process

	Standard Clause	Function/Level	Question	Result
27	8.2.3	Manager	What do you do when planned results are not achieved? *(Examples of correction and corrective action should be provided.)*	
28	8.5.2	Manager	What internal corrective actions have been issued/assigned to or closed in your area(s) since the last internal audit? *(Auditor should randomly sample at least 6 corrective actions.)*	
29	8.5.2	Manager	What customer complaints have been issued/assigned to or closed in your area(s) since the last internal audit? *(Auditor should randomly sample at least 6 customer complaints.)*	

Auditor Name _____   Date of Audit _____

Section 3.2 Customer-Related Process

	Standard Clause	Function/Level	Question	Result
30	8.5.3	Manager	What preventive actions have been issued or closed in your area(s) since the last internal audit? *(Because this number is usually small, the auditor should review all preventive actions.)*	
31	8.5.1	Manager	Please provide examples of continual improvement in your area(s) of responsibility.	
32	4.2.3	All	*Randomly sample at least 8 documents in the area to ensure that they meet requirements of document control procedures. Be sure to include the quality manual, procedures, work instructions, forms, and external documents. Use Appendix B: Documents.*	

Auditor Name _____   Date of Audit _____

Section 3.2 Customer-Related Process

Interview as many customer service reps as possible, asking each one of them questions 32–50 at a minimum:

	Standard Clause	Function/Level	Question	Result
33	4.2.4	Customer service rep	*Randomly sample at least 12 records of contract review in the area to ensure that they meet requirements of record control procedures. Use Appendix C: Records.*	
34	5.1.a	Customer service rep	How does the company communicate the importance of meeting customer, regulatory, and statutory requirements to you?	
35	5.3.d	Customer service rep	What does the quality policy mean to you?	
36	5.4.1	Customer service rep	What are the quality objectives for your area?	

Auditor Name _____   Date of Audit _____

Section 3.2 Customer-Related Process

	Standard Clause	Function/Level	Question	Result
37	5.5.1	Customer service rep	What are your primary responsibilities? *(If not documented, ensure that this matches answer from manager.)*	
38	5.5.1	Customer service rep	Who do you work for? *(Ensure that this matches answer from manager.)*	
39	5.5.3	Customer service rep	How effective is your quality management system? How is this communicated to you?	
40	6.2.2.d	Customer service rep	How do you contribute to the achievement of the quality objectives?	
41	6.2.2.d	Customer service rep	What is the importance of your job?	

Auditor Name _____   Date of Audit _____

Section 3.2 Customer-Related Process

	Standard Clause	Function/Level	Question	Result
42	6.3	Customer service rep	Do you have the equipment and tools you need to do your job?	
43	7.2.2	Customer service rep	What is your process to review the order prior to acceptance? *(The answer should include ensuring that product requirements are defined, resolving any differences, and ensuring that the organization has the ability to meet the requirements.)*	
44	7.2.2	Customer service rep	Who has the authority to review the order to ensure that all requirements can be met?	
45	7.2.2	Customer service rep	What is your record indicating the results of the review?	
46	7.2.2	Customer service rep	What do you do if customers do not provide documentation of their requirements? *(The answer should include a method to confirm customer requirements prior to acceptance.)*	

Auditor Name _____   Date of Audit _____

Section 3.2 Customer-Related Process

	Standard Clause	Function/Level	Question	Result
47	7.2.2	Customer service rep	What happens if an order is changed? *(Ensure that documents are updated and relevant personnel are notified of change.)*	
48	7.2.3	Customer service rep	What is your process to communicate with your customer regarding product information, contracts, customer complaints, etc.?	
49	7.5.4	Customer service rep	What is your record for customer property that is lost, damaged, or otherwise unsuitable for use and to indicate it was reported to the customer? *(Sample all records up to 12.)*	
50	8.5.2 8.5.3	Customer service rep	Have you participated in any corrective and/or preventive actions? If yes, please give an example.	

Auditor Name _____   Date of Audit _____

Section 3.2 Customer-Related Process

	Standard Clause	Function/Level	Question	Result
51	6.1	Determine by observation	*Do resources appear to be adequate to maintain the quality system and continually improve its effectiveness? To enhance customer satisfaction by meeting customer requirements?*	
52	6.3	Determine by observation	*Infrastructure: Does the area include the appropriate workspace, equipment, and supporting services such as communication?*	
53	5.1.a	Supervisor	How do you communicate to your area the importance of meeting customer, regulatory, and statutory requirements?	
54	5.3.d	Supervisor	What does the quality policy mean to you? How do you ensure that the quality policy is communicated and understood?	
55	5.4.1	Supervisor	What are the quality objectives for your area?	

Auditor Name _____   Date of Audit _____

Section 3.2 Customer-Related Process

	Standard Clause	Function/Level	Question	Result
56	5.5.3	Supervisor	What communication processes do you use?	
57	5.5.3	Supervisor	How effective is your quality management system? How do you know?	
58	6.2.2.d	Supervisor	How do you contribute to the achievement of the quality objectives?	
59	6.2.2.d	Supervisor	What is the importance of your job?	
60	6.3	Supervisor	Does your area have the appropriate equipment and tools needed?	

Auditor Name _____   Date of Audit _____

Section 3.2 Customer-Related Process

	Standard Clause	Function/Level	Question	Result
61	7.2.2	Supervisor	What is your process to review the order prior to acceptance? *(The answer should include ensuring that product requirements are defined, resolving any differences, and ensuring that the organization has the ability to meet the requirements.)*	
62	7.2.2	Supervisor	Who has the authority to review the order to ensure that all requirements can be met?	
63	7.2.2	Supervisor	What is your record indicating the results of the review?	
64	7.2.2	Supervisor	What do you do if customers do not provide documentation of their requirements? *(The answer should include a method to confirm customer requirements prior to acceptance.)*	

Auditor Name _____   Date of Audit _____

Section 3.2 Customer-Related Process

	Standard Clause	Function/Level	Question	Result
65	7.2.2	Supervisor	What happens if an order is changed? *(Ensure that documents are updated and relevant personnel are notified of change.)*	
66	7.2.3	Supervisor	What is your process to communicate with your customer regarding product information, contracts, customer complaints, etc.?	

Auditor Name _____   Date of Audit _____

Section 3.2 Customer-Related Process

Use the following section to develop your own questions:

Procedure/Work Instruction	Function/Level	Question	Result

Auditor Name _____   Date of Audit _____

Section 3.3 Design Process

	Standard Clause	Function/Level	Question	Result
1	4.2.3	All	Randomly sample at least 12 documents in the area to ensure that they meet requirements of document control procedures. Be sure to include the quality manual, procedures, work instructions, forms, and external documents. Use Appendix B: Documents.	
2	4.2.4	All	Randomly sample at least 8 records in the area to ensure that they meet requirements of record control procedures. Include records of design input, review, verification, validation, and changes. Use Appendix C: Records.	
3	4.1.a	Manager	What process(es) do you manage?	
4	4.1.b	Manager	How do your processes link with the other processes in the company?	

Auditor Name _____   Date of Audit _____

Section 3.3 Design Process

	Standard Clause	Function/Level	Question	Result
5	5.1.a	Manager	How do you communicate to your area the importance of meeting customer, regulatory, and statutory requirements?	
6	5.3.d	Manager	How do you ensure that the quality policy is communicated and understood?	
7	5.4.1	Manager	What are the quality objectives for your area?	
8	5.4.2	Manager	How do you ensure that the integrity of the quality management system is maintained when changes are planned and implemented?	

Auditor Name _____   Date of Audit _____

Section 3.3 Design Process

	Standard Clause	Function/Level	Question	Result
9	5.5.1	Manager	Where are responsibilities and authorities defined, and how are they communicated?	
10	5.5.3	Manager	What communication processes are established within your area?	
11	5.5.3	Manager	How do you communicate the effectiveness of your quality management system to your area?	
12	6.2.1	Manager	How do you determine competence of your employees?	
13	6.2.2	Manager	What training is required for your employees?	

Auditor Name _____   Date of Audit _____

Section 3.3 Design Process

	Standard Clause	Function/Level	Question	Result
14	6.2.2.d	Manager	How do you ensure that personnel in your area are aware of the importance of their jobs and how they contribute to achievement of quality objectives?	
15	7.1	Manager	How does the design process interact with the planning of product realization as defined by the standard?	
16	7.3.1	Manager	How do you plan and control the design and development of product?	
17	7.3.1	Manager	How do you manage the interfaces between groups involved, to ensure effective communication and clear assignment of responsibility?	

Auditor Name _____   Date of Audit _____

Section 3.3 Design Process

	Standard Clause	Function/Level	Question	Result
18	7.3.1.a 7.3.1.b	Manager	What are your design and development stages? For each stage, what review, verification, and validation are appropriate? *(Response should include software if applicable.)* Stage Review Verification Validation	
19	8.2.1	Manager	What are your customers' perceptions as to whether design has met their requirements? How do you know this?	
20	8.2.3	Manager	What do you do when planned results are not achieved? *(Examples of correction and corrective action should be provided.)*	

Auditor Name _____   Date of Audit _____

Section 3.3 Design Process

	Standard Clause	Function/Level	Question	Result
21	8.2.3 4.1.e	Manager	How do you monitor and measure the design process? Please provide examples.	
22	8.5.1	Manager	Please provide examples of continual improvement in your area(s) of responsibility.	
23	8.5.2	Manager	What internal corrective actions have been issued/assigned to or closed in your area(s) since the last internal audit? *(Auditor should randomly sample at least 6 corrective actions.)*	
24	8.5.2	Manager	What customer complaints have been issued/assigned to or closed in your area(s) since the last internal audit? *(Auditor should randomly sample at least 6 customer complaints.)*	

Auditor Name _____   Date of Audit _____

Section 3.3 Design Process

	Standard Clause	Function/Level	Question	Result
25	8.5.3	Manager	What preventive actions have been issued or closed in your area(s) since the last internal audit? *(Because this number is usually small, the auditor should review all preventive actions.)*	
26	7.3.1.c	Manager	Please explain the responsibilities and authorities for design and development.	
27	5.1.a	Supervisor	How do you communicate to your area the importance of meeting customer, regulatory, and statutory requirements?	
28	5.3.d	Supervisor	What does the quality policy mean to you? How do you ensure that the quality policy is communicated and understood?	

Auditor Name _____   Date of Audit _____

Section 3.3 Design Process

	Standard Clause	Function/Level	Question	Result
29	5.4.1	Supervisor	What are the quality objectives for your area?	
30	5.5.3	Supervisor	What communication processes do you use?	
31	5.5.3	Supervisor	How effective is your quality management system? How do you know?	
32	6.2.2.d	Supervisor	How do you contribute to the achievement of the quality objectives?	
33	6.2.2.d	Supervisor	What is the importance of your job?	
34	6.3	Supervisor	Does your area have the appropriate equipment and tools needed?	

Auditor Name _____   Date of Audit _____

Section 3.3 Design Process

Interview as many design engineers as possible, asking each one of them questions 35–57 at a minimum:

	Standard Clause	Function/Level	Question	Result
35	5.1.a	Design engineer	How does the company communicate the importance of meeting customer, regulatory, and statutory requirements to you?	
36	5.3.d	Design engineer	What does the quality policy mean to you?	
37	5.4.1	Design engineer	What are the quality objectives for your area?	

Auditor Name _____   Date of Audit _____

Section 3.3 Design Process

	Standard Clause	Function/Level	Question	Result
38	5.5.1	Design engineer	What are your primary responsibilities? *(If not documented, ensure that this matches answer from manager.)*	
39	5.5.1	Design engineer	Who do you work for? *(Ensure that this matches answer from manager.)*	
40	5.5.3	Design engineer	How effective is your quality management system? How is this communicated to you?	
41	6.2.2.d	Design engineer	How do you contribute to the achievement of the quality objectives?	
42	6.2.2.d	Design engineer	What is the importance of your job?	

Auditor Name _____   Date of Audit _____

Section 3.3 Design Process

	Standard Clause	Function/Level	Question	Result
43	6.3	Design engineer	Do you have the equipment and tools you need to do your job?	
44	7.3.2	Design engineer	What design projects have you recently completed? Please select several as examples. *(The auditor should randomly select at least one from the list provided by interviewee and ask to see records of design input. Ensure that input includes functional and performance requirements, applicable statutory and regulatory requirements, information obtained from previous similar designs, and other necessary requirements.)*	
45	7.3.2	Design engineer	For each project selected, were inputs reviewed for adequacy?	

Auditor Name _____   Date of Audit _____

Section 3.3 Design Process

	Standard Clause	Function/Level	Question	Result
46	7.3.2	Design engineer	For each project selected, were the requirements complete, clear, and not in conflict with one another?	
47	7.3.3	Design engineer	For each project selected, what are the design outputs? *(Ensure that these outputs meet input requirements, provide information for purchasing and production, contain or reference product acceptance criteria, and specify characteristics of the product essential for its safe and proper use.)*	
48	7.3.3	Design engineer	For each project selected, how were the outputs approved prior to release?	
49	7.3.4	Design engineer	When do design reviews occur?	

Auditor Name _____   Date of Audit _____

Section 3.3 Design Process

	Standard Clause	Function/Level	Question	Result
50	7.3.4	Design engineer	*For each project selected, ask to see records of the results of the review and any necessary actions.*	
51	7.3.4	Design engineer	*Who participated in these reviews? (Ensure that representatives of functions concerned were included.)*	
52	7.3.5	Design engineer	*For each project selected, ask to see records of the results of verification. Ensure verification that design output met design input.*	
53	7.3.6	Design engineer	*For each project selected, ask to see records of validation results. Verify that validation was done to ensure that resulting product was capable of meeting requirements.*	
54	7.3.6	Design engineer	*For each project selected, was validation completed prior to delivery or implementation of the product (if practical)?*	

Auditor Name _____   Date of Audit _____

Section 3.3 Design Process

	Standard Clause	Function/Level	Question	Result
55	7.3.7	Design engineer	*For each project selected, ask to see records of design and development changes. Ensure that each change was reviewed and approved prior to implementation.*	
57	8.5.2 8.5.3	Design engineer	Have you participated in any corrective and/or preventive actions? If yes, please give an example.	
58	6.1	Determine by observation in Design	*Do resources appear to be adequate to maintain the quality system and continually improve its effectiveness? To enhance customer satisfaction by meeting customer requirements?*	
59	6.3	Determine by observation in Design	*Infrastructure: Does the area include the appropriate workspace, equipment, and supporting services such as transport or communication?*	

Auditor Name _____   Date of Audit _____

Section 3.3 Design Process

Interview as many design lab techs as possible, asking each one of them questions 60–74 at a minimum:

	Standard Clause	Function/Level	Question	Result
60	5.1.a	Design lab tech	How does the company communicate the importance of meeting customer, regulatory, and statutory requirements to you?	
61	5.4.1	Design lab tech	What are the quality objectives for your area?	
62	5.5.1	Design lab tech	What are your primary responsibilities? *(If not documented, ensure that this matches answer from manager.)*	
63	5.5.1	Design lab tech	Who do you work for? *(Ensure that this matches answer from manager.)*	

Auditor Name _____   Date of Audit _____

Section 3.3 Design Process

	Standard Clause	Function/Level	Question	Result
64	6.2.2.d	Design lab tech	How do you contribute to the achievement of the quality objectives?	
65	6.2.2.d	Design lab tech	What is the importance of your job?	
66	6.3	Design lab tech	Do you have the equipment and tools you need to do your job?	
67	7.6	Design lab tech	What monitoring and measuring devices do you use in the design lab? *(Sample devices using Appendix D: Calibration.)*	
68	7.6	Design lab tech	How do you know these measuring devices are acceptable to use?	

Auditor Name _____   Date of Audit _____

Section 3.3 Design Process

	Standard Clause	Function/Level	Question	Result
69	8.2.4	Design lab tech	How do you measure new designs to ensure that requirements are met?	
70	8.2.4	Design lab tech	What records do you keep for each project? *(Sample these records for projects sampled from design engineers. Ensure that records demonstrate product/parts met requirements.)*	
71	8.3	Design lab tech	What do you do if a newly designed product or part does not meet requirements?	
72	8.5.2 8.5.3	Design lab tech	Have you participated in any corrective and/or preventive actions? If yes, please give an example.	

Auditor Name _____   Date of Audit _____

Section 3.3 Design Process

	Standard Clause	Function/Level	Question	Result
73	5.3.d	Design lab tech	What does the quality policy mean to you?	
74	5.5.3	Design lab tech	How effective is your quality management system? How is this communicated to you?	
75	6.1	Determine by observation in design lab	*Do resources appear to be adequate to maintain the quality system and continually improve its effectiveness? To enhance customer satisfaction by meeting customer requirements?*	
76	6.3	Determine by observation in design lab	*Infrastructure: Does the area include the appropriate workspace, equipment, and supporting services such as transport or communication?*	

Auditor Name _____   Date of Audit _____

Section 3.3 Design Process

Use the following section to develop your own questions:

Procedure/Work Instruction	Function/Level	Question	Result

Auditor Name _____   Date of Audit _____

Section 3.4 Purchasing Process

	Standard Clause	Function/Level	Question	Result
1	4.2.3	All	*Randomly sample at least 12 documents in the area to ensure that they meet requirements of document control procedures. Be sure to include the quality manual, procedures, work instructions, forms, raw material specifications, and external documents. Use Appendix B: Documents.*	
2	4.2.4	All	*Randomly sample at least 8 records in the area to ensure that they meet requirements of record control procedures. Be sure to include purchase orders, raw material inspection records, certificates of analysis (if used), records of nonconforming raw materials/parts, and supplier evaluations. Use Appendix C: Records.*	
3	4.1.a	Manager	What process(es) do you manage?	
4	4.1.b	Manager	How does your process(es) link with the other processes in the company?	

Auditor Name _____   Date of Audit _____

Section 3.4 Purchasing Process

	Standard Clause	Function/Level	Question	Result
5	5.1.a	Manager	How do you communicate to your area the importance of meeting customer, regulatory, and statutory requirements?	
6	5.3.d	Manager	How do you ensure that the quality policy is communicated and understood?	
7	5.4.1	Manager	What are the quality objectives for your area?	
8	5.4.2	Manager	How do you ensure that the integrity of the quality management system is maintained when changes are planned and implemented?	

Auditor Name _____   Date of Audit _____

Section 3.4 Purchasing Process

	Standard Clause	Function/Level	Question	Result
9	5.5.1	Manager	Where are responsibilities and authorities defined, and how are they communicated?	
10	5.5.3	Manager	What communication processes are established within your area?	
11	5.5.3	Manager	How do you communicate the effectiveness of your quality management system to your area?	
12	6.2.1	Manager	How do you determine competence of your employees?	

Auditor Name _____   Date of Audit _____

Section 3.4 Purchasing Process

	Standard Clause	Function/Level	Question	Result
13	6.2.2.d	Manager	How do you ensure that personnel in your area are aware of the importance of their jobs and how they contribute to achievement of quality objectives?	
14	7.4.1	Manager	How do you make sure purchased product meets specified purchase requirements?	
16	7.4.1	Manager	How do you control your raw material suppliers?	
17	7.4.1	Manager	How do you control other suppliers that impact your product and/or service, such as carriers and providers of calibration services?	

Auditor Name _____   Date of Audit _____

Section 3.4 Purchasing Process

	Standard Clause	Function/Level	Question	Result
18	7.4.1	Manager	How do you select suppliers?	
19	7.4.1	Manager	How do you evaluate and reevaluate suppliers?	
20	7.4.2	Manager	How do you ensure that the purchase requirements are adequate prior to submittal to your supplier?	
21	7.4.3	Manager	How do you ensure that purchased product meets your specified requirements?	
22	7.4.3	Manager	Do you or your customer perform product verification at your supplier's facility? If yes, show me where the arrangements and method of product release are documented in the purchasing information.	

Auditor Name _____   Date of Audit _____

Section 3.4 Purchasing Process

	Standard Clause	Function/Level	Question	Result
23	7.5.5	Manager	Do you receive any raw materials that need special handling, storage, or protection?	
24	8.2.3	Manager	What do you do when planned results are not achieved? *(Examples of correction and corrective action should be provided.)*	
25	8.2.3 4.1.e	Manager	How do you monitor and measure your process? Please provide examples.	
26	8.4.d	Manager	Show me analysis of supplier data.	

Auditor Name _____   Date of Audit _____

Section 3.4 Purchasing Process

	Standard Clause	Function/Level	Question	Result
27	8.5.1	Manager	Please provide examples of continual improvement in your area(s) of responsibility.	
28	8.5.2	Manager	What internal corrective actions have been issued/assigned to or closed in your area(s) since the last internal audit? *(Auditor should randomly sample at least 6 corrective actions.)*	
29	8.5.2	Manager	What customer complaints have been issued/assigned to or closed in your area(s) since the last internal audit? *(Auditor should randomly sample at least 6 customer complaints.)*	
30	8.5.3	Manager	What preventive actions have been issued or closed in your area(s) since the last internal audit? *(Because this number is usually small, the auditor should review all preventive actions.)*	

Auditor Name _____   Date of Audit _____

Section 3.4 Purchasing Process

	Standard Clause	Function/Level	Question	Result
31	7.4	While in Receiving	*Sample raw materials/incoming parts using Appendix A: Purchasing. Complete the form as you go to Purchasing and QC.*	
32	5.1.a	Receiving supervisor	How do you communicate to your area the importance of meeting customer, regulatory, and statutory requirements?	
33	5.3.d	Receiving supervisor	What does the quality policy mean to you? How do you ensure that the quality policy is communicated and understood?	
34	5.4.1	Receiving supervisor	What are the quality objectives for your area?	
35	5.5.3	Receiving supervisor	What communication processes do you use?	

Auditor Name _____   Date of Audit _____

Section 3.4 Purchasing Process

	Standard Clause	Function/Level	Question	Result
36	5.5.3	Receiving supervisor	How effective is your quality management system? How do you know?	
37	6.2.2.d	Receiving supervisor	How do you contribute to the achievement of the quality objectives?	
38	6.2.2.d	Receiving supervisor	What is the importance of your job?	
39	6.3	Receiving supervisor	Does your area have the appropriate equipment and tools needed?	
40	5.3.d	Receiving associate	What does the quality policy mean to you?	

Auditor Name _____   Date of Audit _____

Section 3.4 Purchasing Process

	Standard Clause	Function/Level	Question	Result
41	5.4.1	Receiving associate	What are the quality objectives for your area?	
42	5.5.1	Receiving associate	What are your primary responsibilities? *(If not documented, ensure that this matches answer from manager.)*	
43	5.5.1	Receiving associate	Who do you work for? *(Ensure that this matches answer from manager.)*	
44	5.5.3	Receiving associate	How effective is your quality management system? How is this communicated to you?	
45	6.2.2.d	Receiving associate	How do you contribute to the achievement of the quality objectives?	

Auditor Name _____   Date of Audit _____

Section 3.4 Purchasing Process

	Standard Clause	Function/Level	Question	Result
46	6.2.2.d	Receiving associate	What is the importance of your job?	
47	6.3	Receiving associate	Do you have the equipment and tools you need to do your job?	
48	7.4.2	Receiving associate	What is your process to receive raw materials/parts?	
49	7.5.3	Receiving associate	How are raw materials/parts identified?	
50	7.5.4	Receiving associate	How do you handle customer-owned material and/or parts that are received (if applicable)?	

Auditor Name _____   Date of Audit _____

Section 3.4 Purchasing Process

	Standard Clause	Function/Level	Question	Result
51	7.5.5	Receiving associate	How do you handle and store raw materials/parts?	
52	7.5.5	Receiving associate	Do you receive any raw materials/parts that have special storage and/or protection needs? (*Examples would be temperature requirements such as refrigeration or heat, segregation for explosives, etc. Auditor to follow up with verification.*)	
53	7.6	Receiving associate	Do you use any monitoring and measuring devices? (*If so, sample devices utilizing Appendix D: Calibration.*)	
54	8.2.4	Receiving associate	How do you measure incoming material/parts to ensure that requirements are met?	

Auditor Name _____   Date of Audit _____

Section 3.4 Purchasing Process

	Standard Clause	Function/Level	Question	Result
55	8.3	Receiving associate	What do you do if incoming materials/parts do not meet requirements?	
56	8.5.2 8.5.3	Receiving associate	Have you participated in any corrective and/or preventive actions? If yes, please give an example.	
57	5.1.a	Receiving associate	How does the company communicate the importance of meeting customer, regulatory, and statutory requirements to you?	
58	6.1	Determine by observation in Receiving	*Do resources appear to be adequate to maintain the quality system and continually improve its effectiveness? To enhance customer satisfaction by meeting customer requirements?*	
59	6.3	Determine by observation in Receiving	*Infrastructure: Does the area include the appropriate workspace, equipment, and supporting services such as transport or communication?*	

Auditor Name _____   Date of Audit _____

Section 3.4 Purchasing Process

	Standard Clause	Function/Level	Question	Result
60	6.4	Determine by observation in Receiving	*Is the area's work environment appropriate to meet product requirements?*	
61	5.1.a	Purchasing supervisor	How do you communicate to your area the importance of meeting customer, regulatory, and statutory requirements?	
62	5.3.d	Purchasing supervisor	What does the quality policy mean to you? How do you ensure that the quality policy is communicated and understood?	
63	5.4.1	Purchasing supervisor	What are the quality objectives for your area?	
64	5.5.3	Purchasing supervisor	What communication processes do you use?	

Auditor Name _____   Date of Audit _____

Section 3.4 Purchasing Process

	Standard Clause	Function/Level	Question	Result
65	5.5.3	Purchasing supervisor	How effective is your quality management system? How do you know?	
66	6.2.2.d	Purchasing supervisor	How do you contribute to the achievement of the quality objectives?	
67	6.2.2.d	Purchasing supervisor	What is the importance of your job?	
68	6.3	Purchasing supervisor	Does your area have the appropriate equipment and tools needed?	

Auditor Name _____   Date of Audit _____

Section 3.4 Purchasing Process

Interview as many purchasing associates as possible, asking each one of them questions 69–78 at a minimum:

	Standard Clause	Function/Level	Question	Result
69	5.3.d	Purchasing associate	What does the quality policy mean to you?	
70	5.4.1	Purchasing associate	What are the quality objectives for your area?	
71	6.2.2.d	Purchasing associate	How do you contribute to the achievement of the quality objectives?	
72	6.2.2.d	Purchasing associate	What is the importance of your job?	
73	6.3	Purchasing associate	Do you have the equipment and tools you need to do your job?	
74	8.5.2 8.5.3	Purchasing associate	Have you participated in any corrective and/or preventive actions? If yes, please give an example.	

Auditor Name _____   Date of Audit _____

Section 3.4 Purchasing Process

	Standard Clause	Function/Level	Question	Result
75	5.1.a	Purchasing associate	How does the company communicate the importance of meeting customer, regulatory, and statutory requirements to you?	
76	5.5.1	Purchasing associate	What are your primary responsibilities? *(If not documented, ensure that this matches answer from manager.)*	
77	5.5.1	Purchasing associate	Who do you work for? *(Ensure that this matches answer from manager.)*	
78	5.5.3	Purchasing associate	How effective is your quality management system? How is this communicated to you?	
79	7.4	Purchasing associate	*Continue samples from Appendix A: Purchasing.*	

Auditor Name _____   Date of Audit _____

Section 3.4 Purchasing Process

	Standard Clause	Function/Level	Question	Result
80	6.1	Determine by observation in Purchasing	*Do resources appear to be adequate to maintain the quality system and continually improve its effectiveness? To enhance customer satisfaction by meeting customer requirements?*	
81	6.3	Determine by observation in Purchasing	*Infrastructure: Does the area include the appropriate workspace, equipment, and supporting services such as transport or communication?*	

Interview as many incoming lab/QC techs as possible, asking each one of them questions 82–94 at a minimum:

	Standard Clause	Function/Level	Question	Result
82	5.1.a	Incoming lab/QC tech	How does the company communicate the importance of meeting customer, regulatory, and statutory requirements to you?	
83	5.4.1	Incoming lab/QC tech	What are the quality objectives for your area?	

Auditor Name _____   Date of Audit _____

Section 3.4 Purchasing Process

	Standard Clause	Function/Level	Question	Result
84	5.5.1	Incoming lab/QC tech	What are your primary responsibilities? *(If not documented, ensure that this matches answer from manager.)*	
85	5.5.1	Incoming lab/QC tech	Who do you work for? *(Ensure that this matches answer from manager.)*	
86	6.2.2.d	Incoming lab/QC tech	How do you contribute to the achievement of the quality objectives?	
87	6.2.2.d	Incoming lab/QC tech	What is the importance of your job?	
88	6.3	Incoming lab/QC tech	Do you have the equipment and tools you need to do your job?	
89	7.5.6	Incoming lab/QC tech	What monitoring and measuring devices do you use to test raw material/incoming parts? *(Sample devices using Appendix D: Calibration.)*	

Auditor Name _____   Date of Audit _____

Section 3.4 Purchasing Process

	Standard Clause	Function/Level	Question	Result
90	7.6	Incoming lab/QC tech	How do you know this measuring device is acceptable to use?	
91	8.2.4	Incoming lab/QC tech	How do you measure incoming material/parts to ensure that requirements are met?	
92	8.2.4	Incoming lab/QC tech	What records do you keep? *(Ensure records demonstrate that product/parts met requirements and indicate who authorized release; utilize Appendix A: Purchasing.)*	
93	8.3	Incoming lab/QC tech	What do you do if incoming materials/parts do not meet requirements?	

Auditor Name _____   Date of Audit _____

Section 3.4 Purchasing Process

	Standard Clause	Function/Level	Question	Result
94	8.5.2 8.5.3	Incoming lab/QC tech	Have you participated in any corrective and/or preventive actions? If yes, please give an example.	
95	5.3.d	Incoming lab/QC tech	What does the quality policy mean to you?	
96	5.5.3	Incoming lab/QC tech	How effective is your quality management system? How is this communicated to you?	
97	6.1	Determine by observation in incoming lab/QC	Do resources appear to be adequate to maintain the quality system and continually improve its effectiveness? To enhance customer satisfaction by meeting customer requirements?	
98	6.3	Determine by observation in incoming lab/QC	Infrastructure: Does the area include the appropriate workspace, equipment, and supporting services such as transport or communication?	
99	6.4	Determine by observation in incoming lab/QC	Is the area's work environment appropriate to meet product requirements?	

Auditor Name _____   Date of Audit _____

Section 3.4 Purchasing Process

Use the following section to develop your own questions:

Procedure/Work Instruction	Function/Level	Question	Result

Auditor Name _____   Date of Audit _____

Section 3.5 Production Process

	Standard Clause	Function/Level	Question	Result
1	4.1.a	Production manager	What process(es) do you manage?	
2	4.1.b	Production manager	How does your process(es) link with the other processes in the company?	
3	5.1.a	Production manager	How do you communicate to your area the importance of meeting customer, regulatory, and statutory requirements?	
4	5.3.d	Production manager	How do you ensure that the quality policy is communicated and understood?	

Auditor Name _____   Date of Audit _____

Section 3.5 Production Process

	Standard Clause	Function/Level	Question	Result
5	5.4.1	Production manager	What are the quality objectives for your area?	
6	5.4.2	Production manager	How do you ensure that the integrity of the quality management system is maintained when changes are planned and implemented?	
7	5.5.1	Production manager	Where are responsibilities and authorities defined, and how are they communicated?	
8	5.5.3	Production manager	What communication processes are established within your area?	
9	5.5.3	Production manager	How do you communicate the effectiveness of your quality management system to your area?	

Auditor Name _____   Date of Audit _____

Section 3.5 Production Process

	Standard Clause	Function/Level	Question	Result
10	6.2.1	Production manager	How do you determine competence of your employees?	
11	6.2.2.d	Production manager	How do you ensure that personnel in your area are aware of the importance of their jobs and how they contribute to achievement of quality objectives?	
12	7.1	Production manager	How do you plan product realization?	
13	7.2.2	Production manager	When a customer order is amended, how is this communicated with Production?	
14	7.2.2	Production manager	When customer requirements are changed, how is this communicated with Production?	

Auditor Name _____   Date of Audit _____

Section 3.5 Production Process

	Standard Clause	Function/Level	Question	Result
15	7.3	Production manager	How does the Production department interact with the group responsible for design?	
16	7.5.1	Production manager	How are production processes controlled?	
17	7.5.1.a	Production manager	Where do you find information about product characteristics?	
18	7.5.1.b	Production manager	Does your area use work instructions? What format are they in?	
19	7.5.2	Production manager	Do you have any production processes where the resulting output cannot be verified by subsequent monitoring or measurement ("special" processes such as welding)? If so, how do you validate and revalidate these processes per 7.5.2 of the standard?	

Auditor Name _____   Date of Audit _____

Section 3.5 Production Process

	Standard Clause	Function/Level	Question	Result
20	7.5.3	Production manager	How is product identified in your areas?	
21	7.5.3	Production manager	Is traceability required? If yes, how is this done and what is the record of unique product identification?	
22	7.5.3	Production manager	*If traceability is required, the auditor should randomly sample a minimum of 6 products that shipped since the last internal audit. Trace each of these products back to the raw materials/incoming parts used. Ask the production manager to provide someone to assist you when you finish with the production manager's interview.*	

Auditor Name _____   Date of Audit _____

Section 3.5 Production Process

	Standard Clause	Function/Level	Question	Result
23	7.5.4	Production manager	Do you have any customer property? If yes, how is it controlled? If it is lost, damaged, or otherwise unsuitable for use, how is this reported to the customer? What is the record?	
24	7.5.5	Production manager	How is product preserved during production and delivery?	
24a	7.5.5	Production manager	How is expired material identified and quarantined on the manufacturing floor?	
25	7.5.5	Production manager	What controls do you have in place for proper handling, packaging, storage, and protection of product?	
26	8.2.1 8.4	Production manager	What are your customers' perceptions as to whether your product has met their requirements? What data does your area collect and analyze pertaining to customer satisfaction?	

Auditor Name _____   Date of Audit _____

Section 3.5 Production Process

	Standard Clause	Function/Level	Question	Result
27	8.2.3	Production manager	What do you do when planned results are not achieved? *(Examples of correction and corrective action should be provided.)*	
28	8.2.3 4.1.e	Production manager	How do you monitor and measure your process? Please provide examples. *(The response should include data pertaining to characteristics and trends of process.)*	
29	8.2.4	Production manager	How do you monitor and measure your product? What records are kept as evidence of conformity? What records are kept to indicate who authorized release? *(The response should include data pertaining to characteristics and trends of product.)*	
30	8.3	Production manager	What is your process to control nonconforming product?	

Auditor Name _____   Date of Audit _____

Section 3.5 Production Process

	Standard Clause	Function/Level	Question	Result
31	8.4	Production manager	What data does your area collect and analyze pertaining to opportunities for preventive actions?	
32	8.5.1	Production manager	Please provide examples of continual improvement in your area(s) of responsibility.	
33	8.5.2	Production manager	What internal corrective actions have been issued/assigned to or closed in your area(s) since the last internal audit? *(Auditor should randomly sample at least 6 corrective actions.)*	
34	8.5.2	Production manager	What customer complaints have been issued/assigned to or closed in your area(s) since the last internal audit? *(Auditor should randomly sample at least 6 customer complaints.)*	

Auditor Name _____   Date of Audit _____

Section 3.5 Production Process

	Standard Clause	Function/Level	Question	Result
35	8.5.3	Production manager	What preventive actions have been issued or closed in your area(s) since the last internal audit? *(Because this number is usually small, the auditor should review all preventive actions.)*	
36	8.5.2 8.5.3	Production supervisor/team leader	Have you participated in any corrective and/or preventive actions? If yes, please give an example.	
37	5.1.a	Production supervisor/team leader	How do you communicate to your area the importance of meeting customer, regulatory, and statutory requirements?	
38	5.3.d	Production supervisor/team leader	What does the quality policy mean to you? How do you ensure that the quality policy is communicated and understood?	
39	5.4.1	Production supervisor/team leader	What are the quality objectives for your area?	

Auditor Name _____   Date of Audit _____

Section 3.5 Production Process

	Standard Clause	Function/Level	Question	Result
40	5.5.3	Production supervisor/team leader	What communication processes do you use?	
41	5.5.3	Production supervisor/team leader	How effective is your quality management system? How do you know?	
42	6.2.2.d	Production supervisor/team leader	How do you contribute to the achievement of the quality objectives?	
43	6.2.2.d	Production supervisor/team leader	What is the importance of your job?	
44	6.3	Production supervisor/team leader	Does your area have the appropriate equipment and tools needed?	

Auditor Name _____   Date of Audit _____

Section 3.5 Production Process

	Standard Clause	Function/Level	Question	Result
45	7.2.2	Production supervisor/team leader	When a customer order is amended, how is this communicated with Production?	
46	7.2.2	Production supervisor/team leader	When customer requirements are changed, how is this communicated with Production?	
47	7.5.1	Production supervisor/team leader	How are production processes controlled?	
48	7.5.1.a	Production supervisor/team leader	Where do you find information about product characteristics?	
49	7.5.1.b	Production supervisor/team leader	Does your area use work instructions? What format are they in?	

Auditor Name _____   Date of Audit _____

Section 3.5 Production Process

	Standard Clause	Function/Level	Question	Result
50	7.5.2	Production supervisor/team leader	Do you have any production processes where the resulting output cannot be verified by subsequent monitoring or measurement ("special" processes such as welding)? If so, how do you validate and revalidate these processes per 7.5.2 of the standard?	
51	7.5.2	Production supervisor/team leader	If the area has "special" processes, the auditor should sample each process to ensure that it is properly controlled: 1. The process must be reviewed and approved based on defined criteria. 2. The equipment must be approved. 3. The persons working on it must be qualified. 4. There must be work instructions of some type. 5. The process must be revalidated. 6. There should be records for each of the above.	

Auditor Name _____   Date of Audit _____

Section 3.5 Production Process

	Standard Clause	Function/Level	Question	Result
52	7.5.3	Production supervisor/team leader	How is product identified in your areas?	
53	7.5.4	Production supervisor/team leader	Do you have any customer property? If yes, how is it controlled? If it is lost, damaged, or otherwise unsuitable for use, how is this reported to the customer? What is the record?	
54	7.5.5	Production supervisor/team leader	How is product preserved during production?	
55	7.5.5	Production supervisor/team leader	What controls do you have in place for proper handling, packaging, storage, and protection of product?	
56	8.3	Production supervisor/team leader	What is your process to control nonconforming product?	

Auditor Name _____   Date of Audit _____

Section 3.5 Production Process

	Standard Clause	Function/Level	Question	Result
57	8.3	Production supervisor/team leader	Do you rework product? If so, how is it reverified? *(Sample to ensure that this is done.)*	

Interview as many production associates as possible, asking each one of them questions 58–75 at a minimum:

	Standard Clause	Function/Level	Question	Result
58	5.1.a	Production associate	How does the company communicate the importance of meeting customer, regulatory, and statutory requirements to you?	
59	5.3.d	Production associate	What does the quality policy mean to you?	
60	5.4.1	Production associate	What are the quality objectives for your area?	

Auditor Name _____   Date of Audit _____

Section 3.5 Production Process

	Standard Clause	Function/Level	Question	Result
61	5.5.1	Production associate	What are your primary responsibilities? *(If not documented, ensure that this matches answer from manager.)*	
62	5.5.1	Production associate	Who do you work for? *(Ensure that this matches answer from manager.)*	
63	5.5.3	Production associate	How effective is your quality management system? How is this communicated to you?	
64	6.2.2.d	Production associate	How do you contribute to the achievement of the quality objectives?	
65	6.2.2.d	Production associate	What is the importance of your job?	

Auditor Name _____   Date of Audit _____

Section 3.5 Production Process

	Standard Clause	Function/Level	Question	Result
66	6.3	Production associate	Do you have the equipment and tools you need to do your job?	
67	8.5.2 8.5.3	Production associate	Have you participated in any corrective and/or preventive actions? If yes, please give an example.	
68	7.5.1	Production associate	What process parameters do you monitor? What records do you keep? *(Auditor should verify that actual process settings match requirements. Use additional sheets if necessary.)* Parameter Actual Setting Required Setting	

Auditor Name _____   Date of Audit _____

Section 3.5 Production Process

	Standard Clause	Function/Level	Question	Result
69	7.5.1.b	Production associate	Show me your work instructions.	
70	7.5.3	Production associate	What product are you running and how is it identified?	
71	7.5.5	Production associate	Does the product that you're running [name of product: _____] have any requirements for: Handling? Packaging? Storage? Protection?	

Auditor Name _____   Date of Audit _____

Section 3.5 Production Process

	Standard Clause	Function/Level	Question	Result
72	7.6	Production associate	For the product that you're running [name of product: _____], what monitoring and measuring devices do you use? Be certain to include both product and process measuring devices as applicable. *(Record these instruments using Appendix D: Calibration.)*	
73	7.6	Production associate	How do you know this measuring device is acceptable to use?	
74	8.2.	Production associate	For the product that you're running [name of product: _____], how do you monitor and/or measure the product? *(Verify that answer is correct and that measurements were taken at appropriate frequency and were within spec.)*	
75	8.3	Production associate	What do you do if you find product out of specification? What happens to the product?	

Auditor Name _____   Date of Audit _____

Section 3.5 Production Process

	Standard Clause	Function/Level	Question	Result
76	6.1	Determine by observation in Production	*Do resources appear to be adequate to maintain the quality system and continually improve its effectiveness? To enhance customer satisfaction by meeting customer requirements?*	
77	6.3	Determine by observation in Production	*Infrastructure: Does the area include the appropriate workspace, equipment, and supporting services such as transport or communication?*	
78	6.4	Determine by observation in Production	*Is the area's work environment appropriate to meet product requirements?*	
79	4.2.3	All–Production	*Randomly sample at least 12 documents in the area to ensure that they meet requirements of document control procedures. Be sure to include the quality manual, procedures, work instructions, forms, product specifications/drawings, and external documents. Use Appendix B: Documents.*	
80	4.2.4	All–Production	*Randomly sample at least 8 records in the area to ensure that they meet requirements of record control procedures. Use Appendix C: Records.*	

Auditor Name _____   Date of Audit _____

Section 3.5 Production Process

	Standard Clause	Function/Level	Question	Result
81	4.2.3	All–Lab	*Randomly sample at least 12 documents in the area to ensure that they meet requirements of document control procedures. Be sure to include the quality manual, procedures, work instructions, forms, product specifications/drawings, and external documents. Use Appendix B: Documents.*	
82	4.2.4	All–Lab	*Randomly sample at least 8 records in the area to ensure that they meet requirements of record control procedures. Use Appendix C: Records.*	
83	6.1	Determine by observation in lab	*Do resources appear to be adequate to maintain the quality system and continually improve its effectiveness? To enhance customer satisfaction by meeting customer requirements?*	
84	6.3	Determine by observation in lab	*Infrastructure: Does the area include the appropriate workspace, equipment, and supporting services such as transport or communication?*	
85	6.4	Determine by observation in lab	*Is the area's work environment appropriate to meet product requirements?*	
86	4.1.a	Lab manager	What process(es) do you manage?	

Auditor Name _____   Date of Audit _____

Section 3.5 Production Process

	Standard Clause	Function/Level	Question	Result
87	4.1.b	Lab manager	How does your process(es) link with the other processes in the company?	
88	5.1.a	Lab manager	How do you communicate to your area the importance of meeting customer, regulatory, and statutory requirements?	
89	5.3.d	Lab manager	How do you ensure that the quality policy is communicated and understood?	
90	5.4.1	Lab manager	What are the quality objectives for your area?	

Auditor Name _____   Date of Audit _____

Section 3.5 Production Process

	Standard Clause	Function/Level	Question	Result
91	5.4.2	Lab manager	How do you ensure that the integrity of the quality management system is maintained when changes are planned and implemented?	
92	5.5.1	Lab manager	Where are responsibilities and authorities defined, and how are they communicated?	
93	5.5.3	Lab manager	What communication processes are established within your area?	
94	5.5.3	Lab manager	How do you communicate the effectiveness of your quality management system to your area?	
95	6.2.1	Lab manager	How do you determine competence of your employees?	

Auditor Name _____   Date of Audit _____

Section 3.5 Production Process

	Standard Clause	Function/Level	Question	Result
96	6.2.2.d	Lab manager	How do you ensure that personnel in your area are aware of the importance of their jobs and how they contribute to achievement of quality objectives?	
97	7.6	Lab manager	Is your area responsible for calibrations/verifications in the lab? In the plant?	
98	8.2.3	Lab manager	What do you do when planned results are not achieved? *(Examples of correction and corrective action should be provided.)*	
99	8.2.3 4.1.e	Lab manager	How do you monitor and measure your process? Please provide examples.	

Auditor Name _____   Date of Audit _____

Section 3.5 Production Process

	Standard Clause	Function/Level	Question	Result
100	8.3	Lab manager	What is your process to control nonconforming product?	
101	8.3	Lab manager	How is nonconforming product identified and tracked?	
102	8.3	Lab manager	What is your record of nonconformity and subsequent actions taken, including concessions?	
103	8.3	Lab manager	What do you do if nonconforming product is found after delivery or use has started?	

Auditor Name _____   Date of Audit _____

Section 3.5 Production Process

	Standard Clause	Function/Level	Question	Result
104	8.5.1	Lab manager	Please provide examples of continual improvement in your area(s) of responsibility.	
105	8.5.2	Lab manager	What internal corrective actions have been issued/assigned to or closed in your area(s) since the last internal audit? *(Auditor should randomly sample at least 6 corrective actions.)*	
106	8.5.2	Lab manager	What customer complaints have been issued/assigned to or closed in your area(s) since the last internal audit? *(Auditor should randomly sample at least 6 customer complaints.)*	
107	8.5.3	Lab manager	What preventive actions have been issued or closed in your area(s) since the last internal audit? *(Because this number is usually small, the auditor should review all preventive actions.)*	

Auditor Name _____   Date of Audit _____

Section 3.5 Production Process

	Standard Clause	Function/Level	Question	Result
108	5.1.a	Lab supervisor/team leader	How do you communicate to your area the importance of meeting customer, regulatory, and statutory requirements?	
109	5.3.d	Lab supervisor/team leader	What does the quality policy mean to you? How do you ensure that the quality policy is communicated and understood?	
110	5.4.1	Lab supervisor/team leader	What are the quality objectives for your area?	
111	5.5.3	Lab supervisor/team leader	What communication processes do you use?	
112	5.5.3	Lab supervisor/team leader	How effective is your quality management system? How do you know?	

Auditor Name _____   Date of Audit _____

Section 3.5 Production Process

	Standard Clause	Function/Level	Question	Result
113	6.2.2.d	Lab supervisor/team leader	How do you contribute to the achievement of the quality objectives?	
114	6.2.2.d	Lab supervisor/team leader	What is the importance of your job?	
115	6.3	Lab supervisor/team leader	Does your area have the appropriate equipment and tools needed?	
116	7.5.3	Lab supervisor/team leader	How are samples and/or parts identified while in the lab?	
117	7.6	Lab supervisor/team leader	Do you use any outside calibration companies? *(If yes, add to list of suppliers in Appendix A: Purchasing.)*	

Auditor Name _____   Date of Audit _____

Section 3.5 Production Process

	Standard Clause	Function/Level	Question	Result
118	7.6	Lab supervisor/team leader	*For samples that the lab is responsible for (collected on Appendix D: Calibration), the auditor should ensure that all calibration requirements are met for each instrument. Be sure each instrument was checked against standards traceable to international or national measurement standards. Or if there is no such standard, the basis for calibration/verification must be recorded. Add internal standards used to Appendix D: Calibration. Be sure to sample both instruments that were calibrated and verified internally and those calibrated by an outside supplier. If any other outside calibration suppliers are found but not mentioned previously during the audit, be sure to add them to Appendix A: Purchasing.*	
119	7.6	Lab supervisor/team leader	How do you ensure that monitoring and measurement devices are protected during handling, maintenance, and storage?	
120	7.6	Lab supervisor/team leader	What do you do if an instrument does not conform to requirements? *(The auditor must verify that the validity of previous measuring results is assessed and recorded. There should be evidence that the proper action was taken on the instrument and any product affected.)*	

Auditor Name _____   Date of Audit _____

Section 3.5 Production Process

	Standard Clause	Function/Level	Question	Result
121	8.3	Lab supervisor/team leader	What is your process to control nonconforming product?	
122	8.3	Lab supervisor/team leader	*Auditor should randomly select at least 6 products identified as nonconforming product since the last internal audit. Ensure that procedures for nonconforming product were followed for each. Ensure that appropriate concessions were obtained if applicable.*	
123	8.3	Lab supervisor/team leader	What nonconforming product is currently in-house? *(Auditor should randomly choose nonconforming product and ensure that it is properly identified.)*	

Auditor Name _____   Date of Audit _____

Section 3.5 Production Process

Interview as many incoming lab techs as possible, asking each one of them questions 124–139 at a minimum:

	Standard Clause	Function/Level	Question	Result
124	5.1.a	Lab tech	How does the company communicate the importance of meeting customer, regulatory, and statutory requirements to you?	
125	5.3.d	Lab tech	What does the quality policy mean to you?	
126	5.4.1	Lab tech	What are the quality objectives for your area?	
127	5.5.1	Lab tech	What are your primary responsibilities? *(If not documented, ensure that this matches answer from manager.)*	

Auditor Name _____   Date of Audit _____

Section 3.5 Production Process

	Standard Clause	Function/Level	Question	Result
128	5.5.1	Lab tech	Who do you work for? *(Ensure that this matches answer from manager.)*	
129	5.5.3	Lab tech	How effective is your quality management system? How is this communicated to you?	
130	6.2.2.d	Lab tech	How do you contribute to the achievement of the quality objectives?	
131	6.2.2.d	Lab tech	What is the importance of your job?	
132	6.3	Lab tech	Do you have the equipment and tools you need to do your job?	

Auditor Name _____   Date of Audit _____

Section 3.5 Production Process

	Standard Clause	Function/Level	Question	Result
133	7.5.3	Lab tech	What sample or part are you working on now? How is it identified while in the lab? Name of product: _____	
134	7.6	Lab tech	What monitoring and measuring devices are used for this product? *(Record the instruments using Appendix D: Calibration.)*	
135	7.6	Lab tech	How do you know these measuring devices are acceptable to use?	
136	8.2.4	Lab tech	What tests and/or measurements are required for this product? How do you know this?	

Auditor Name _____   Date of Audit _____

Section 3.5 Production Process

	Standard Clause	Function/Level	Question	Result
137	8.2.4	Lab tech	*Ask the lab tech to show you the records from previous test results. Randomly select records from at least 6 runs since the last internal audit (attach additional sheets if necessary). Ensure that all required tests were performed, and all results were within specification.*	
138	8.3	Lab tech	What do you do when product is found outside specification?	
139	8.5.2 8.5.3	Lab tech	Have you participated in any corrective and/or preventive actions? If yes, please give an example.	
140	4.2.4	All– Maintenance	*Randomly sample at least 6 records in the area to ensure that they meet requirements of record control procedures. Use Appendix C: Records.*	

Auditor Name _____   Date of Audit _____

Section 3.5 Production Process

	Standard Clause	Function/Level	Question	Result
141	4.2.3	All– Maintenance	*Randomly sample at least 6 documents in the area to ensure that they meet requirements of document control procedures. Be sure to include the quality manual, procedures, work instructions, forms, and external documents. Use Appendix B: Documents.*	
142	6.1	Determine by observation in Maintenance	*Do resources appear to be adequate to maintain the quality system and continually improve its effectiveness? To enhance customer satisfaction by meeting customer requirements?*	
143	6.3	Determine by observation in Maintenance	*Infrastructure: Does the area include the appropriate workspace, equipment, and supporting services such as transport or communication?*	
144	6.4	Determine by observation in Maintenance	*Is the area's work environment appropriate to meet product requirements?*	
145	4.1.a	Maintenance manager	What process(es) do you manage?	

Auditor Name _____   Date of Audit _____

Section 3.5 Production Process

	Standard Clause	Function/Level	Question	Result
146	8.2.3 4.1.e	Maintenance manager	How do you monitor and measure your processes? Please provide examples.	
147	4.1.b	Maintenance manager	How does your process(es) link with the other processes in the company?	
148	5.1.a	Maintenance manager	How do you communicate to your area the importance of meeting customer, regulatory, and statutory requirements?	
149	5.3.d	Maintenance manager	How do you ensure that the quality policy is communicated and understood?	

Auditor Name _____   Date of Audit _____

Section 3.5 Production Process

	Standard Clause	Function/Level	Question	Result
150	5.4.1	Maintenance manager	What are the quality objectives for your area?	
151	5.5.1	Maintenance manager	Where are responsibilities and authorities defined, and how are they communicated?	
152	5.4.2	Maintenance manager	How do you ensure that the integrity of the quality management system is maintained when changes are planned and implemented?	
153	5.5.3	Maintenance manager	What communication processes are established within your area?	

Auditor Name _____   Date of Audit _____

Section 3.5 Production Process

	Standard Clause	Function/Level	Question	Result
154	5.5.3	Maintenance manager	How do you communicate the effectiveness of your quality management system to your area?	
155	6.2.1	Maintenance manager	How do you determine competence of your employees?	
156	6.2.2.d	Maintenance manager	How do you ensure that personnel in your area are aware of the importance of their jobs and how they contribute to achievement of quality objectives?	
157	7.5.1	Maintenance manager	Explain your process for maintenance/preventive maintenance.	

Auditor Name _____   Date of Audit _____

Section 3.5 Production Process

	Standard Clause	Function/Level	Question	Result
158	7.5.1	Maintenance manager	How do you manage past due work orders?	
159	8.2.3	Maintenance manager	What do you do when planned results are not achieved? *(Examples of correction and corrective action should be provided.)*	
160	8.5.1	Maintenance manager	Please provide examples of continual improvement in your area(s) of responsibility.	
161	8.5.2	Maintenance manager	What internal corrective actions have been issued/assigned to or closed in your area(s) since the last internal audit? *(Auditor should randomly sample at least 6 corrective actions.)*	

Auditor Name _____   Date of Audit _____

Section 3.5 Production Process

	Standard Clause	Function/Level	Question	Result
162	8.5.3	Maintenance manager	What preventive actions have been issued or closed in your area(s) since the last internal audit? *(Because this number is usually small, the auditor should review all preventive actions.)*	
163	5.1.a	Maintenance supervisor/team leader	How do you communicate to your area the importance of meeting customer, regulatory, and statutory requirements?	
164	5.3.d	Maintenance supervisor/team leader	What does the quality policy mean to you? How do you ensure that the quality policy is communicated and understood?	
165	5.4.1	Maintenance supervisor/team leader	What are the quality objectives for your area?	
166	5.5.3	Maintenance supervisor/team leader	What communication processes do you use?	

Auditor Name _____ Date of Audit _____

Section 3.5 Production Process

	Standard Clause	Function/Level	Question	Result
167	5.5.3	Maintenance supervisor/team leader	How effective is your quality management system? How do you know?	
168	6.3	Maintenance supervisor/team leader	Does your area have the appropriate equipment and tools needed?	
169	6.2.2.d	Maintenance supervisor/team leader	How do you contribute to the achievement of the quality objectives?	
170	6.2.2.d	Maintenance supervisor/team leader	What is the importance of your job?	
171	7.5.1	Maintenance supervisor/team leader	Explain your process for maintenance/preventive maintenance.	

Auditor Name _____ Date of Audit _____

Section 3.5 Production Process

	Standard Clause	Function/Level	Question	Result
172	7.5.1	Maintenance supervisor/team leader	What do you do when work orders are past due?	
173	7.6	Maintenance supervisor/team leader	*For samples that Maintenance is responsible for (collected on Appendix D: Calibration), the auditor should ensure that all calibration requirements are met for each instrument. Be sure each instrument was checked against standards traceable to international or national measurement standards. Or if there is no such standard, the basis for calibration/verification must be recorded. Add internal standards used to Appendix D: Calibration. Be sure to sample instruments calibrated and verified internally as well as those calibrated by an external supplier. Add external providers of calibration services to Appendix A: Purchasing.*	
174	7.6	Maintenance supervisor/team leader	How do you ensure that monitoring and measurement devices are protected during handling, maintenance, and storage?	

Auditor Name _____   Date of Audit _____

Section 3.5 Production Process

	Standard Clause	Function/Level	Question	Result
175	7.6	Maintenance supervisor/team leader	What do you do if an instrument does not conform to requirements? *(The auditor must verify that the validity of previous measuring results is assessed and recorded. There should be evidence that the proper action was taken on the instrument and any product affected.)*	
176	5.1.a	Maintenance tech	How does the company communicate the importance of meeting customer, regulatory, and statutory requirements to you?	
177	5.3.d	Maintenance tech	What does the quality policy mean to you?	
178	5.4.1	Maintenance tech	What are the quality objectives for your area?	

Auditor Name _____   Date of Audit _____

Section 3.5 Production Process

	Standard Clause	Function/Level	Question	Result
179	5.5.1	Maintenance tech	What are your primary responsibilities? *(If not documented, ensure that this matches answer from manager.)*	
180	5.5.1	Maintenance tech	Who do you work for? *(Ensure that this matches answer from manager.)*	
181	5.5.3	Maintenance tech	How effective is your quality management system? How is this communicated to you?	
182	6.3	Maintenance tech	Do you have the equipment and tools you need to do your job?	
183	6.2.2.d	Maintenance tech	How do you contribute to the achievement of the quality objectives?	
184	6.2.2.d	Maintenance tech	What is the importance of your job?	

Auditor Name _____   Date of Audit _____

Section 3.5 Production Process

	Standard Clause	Function/Level	Question	Result
185	7.5.1	Maintenance tech	How do you know what is required for a PM (preventive maintenance)?	
186	8.5.2 8.5.3	Maintenance tech	Have you participated in any corrective and/or preventive actions? If yes, please give an example.	
187	4.1.a	Shipping manager	What process(es) do you manage?	
188	4.1.b	Shipping manager	How does your process(es) link with the other processes in the company?	
189	5.1.a	Shipping manager	How do you communicate to your area the importance of meeting customer, regulatory, and statutory requirements?	

Auditor Name _____   Date of Audit _____

Section 3.5 Production Process

	Standard Clause	Function/Level	Question	Result
190	5.3.d	Shipping manager	How do you ensure that the quality policy is communicated and understood?	
191	5.4.1	Shipping manager	What are the quality objectives for your area?	
192	5.4.2	Shipping manager	How do you ensure that the integrity of the quality management system is maintained when changes are planned and implemented?	
193	5.5.1	Shipping manager	How are responsibilities and authorities defined, and how are they communicated?	
194	5.5.3	Shipping manager	What communication processes are established within your area?	

Auditor Name _____   Date of Audit _____

Section 3.5 Production Process

	Standard Clause	Function/Level	Question	Result
195	5.5.3	Shipping manager	How do you communicate the effectiveness of your quality management system to your area?	
196	6.2.1	Shipping manager	How do you determine competence of your employees?	
197	6.2.2.d	Shipping manager	How do you ensure that that personnel in your area are aware of the importance of their jobs and how they contribute to achievement of quality objectives?	
198	7.2.2	Shipping manager	When customer requirements are changed, how is this communicated with Shipping?	
199	7.5.3	Shipping manager	How is product identified in your areas?	

Auditor Name _____   Date of Audit _____

Section 3.5 Production Process

	Standard Clause	Function/Level	Question	Result
200	7.5.5	Shipping manager	How is product preserved during storage and delivery?	
201	7.5.5	Shipping manager	What controls do you have in place for proper handling, packaging, storage, and protection of product?	
202	8.2.3	Shipping manager	What do you do when planned results are not achieved? *(Examples of correction and corrective action should be provided.)*	
203	8.2.3 4.1.e	Shipping manager	How do you monitor and measure your process? Please provide examples. *(Response should include data pertaining to characteristics and trends of process.)*	

Auditor Name _____   Date of Audit _____

Section 3.5 Production Process

	Standard Clause	Function/Level	Question	Result
204	8.4	Shipping manager	What data does your area collect and analyze pertaining to opportunities for preventive actions?	
205	8.5.1	Shipping manager	Please provide examples of continual improvement in your area(s) of responsibility.	
206	8.5.2	Shipping manager	What internal corrective actions have been issued/assigned to or closed in your area(s) since the last internal audit? *(Auditor should randomly sample at least 6 corrective actions.)*	
207	8.5.2	Shipping manager	What customer complaints have been issued/assigned to or closed in your area(s) since the last internal audit? *(Auditor should randomly sample at least 6 customer complaints.)*	

Auditor Name _____   Date of Audit _____

Section 3.5 Production Process

	Standard Clause	Function/Level	Question	Result
208	8.5.3	Shipping manager	What preventive actions have been issued or closed in your area(s) since the last internal audit? *(Because this number is usually small, the auditor should review all preventive actions.)*	
209	8.5.2 8.5.3	Shipping supervisor/team leader	Have you participated in any corrective and/or preventive actions? If yes, please give an example.	
210	5.1.a	Shipping supervisor/team leader	How do you communicate to your area the importance of meeting customer, regulatory, and statutory requirements?	
211	5.3.d	Shipping supervisor/team leader	What does the quality policy mean to you? How do you ensure that the quality policy is communicated and understood?	
212	5.4.1	Shipping supervisor/team leader	What are the quality objectives for your area?	

Auditor Name _____   Date of Audit _____

Section 3.5 Production Process

	Standard Clause	Function/Level	Question	Result
213	5.5.3	Shipping supervisor/team leader	What communication processes do you use?	
214	5.5.3	Shipping supervisor/team leader	How effective is your quality management system? How do you know?	
215	6.2.2.d	Shipping supervisor/team leader	How do you contribute to the achievement of the quality objectives?	
216	6.2.2.d	Shipping supervisor/team leader	What is the importance of your job?	
217	6.3	Shipping supervisor/team leader	Does your area have the appropriate equipment and tools needed?	

Auditor Name _____   Date of Audit _____

Section 3.5 Production Process

	Standard Clause	Function/Level	Question	Result
218	7.2.2	Shipping supervisor/team leader	When a customer order is amended, how is this communicated with Shipping?	
219	7.2.2	Shipping supervisor/team leader	When customer requirements are changed, how is this communicated with Shipping?	
220	7.4	Shipping supervisor/team leader	Which carriers do you use? (Use Appendix A: Purchasing.)	
221	7.5.3	Shipping supervisor/team leader	How is product identified in your areas?	
222	7.5.5	Shipping supervisor/team leader	How is product preserved during storage and delivery?	

Auditor Name _____   Date of Audit _____

Section 3.5 Production Process

	Standard Clause	Function/Level	Question	Result
223	7.5.5	Shipping supervisor/team leader	What controls do you have in place for proper handling, packaging, storage, and protection of product?	
224	5.1.a	Shipping associate	How does the company communicate the importance of meeting customer, regulatory, and statutory requirements to you?	
225	5.3.d	Shipping associate	What does the quality policy mean to you?	
226	5.4.1	Shipping associate	What are the quality objectives for your area?	
227	5.5.1	Shipping associate	What are your primary responsibilities? (If not documented, ensure that this matches answer from manager.)	

Auditor Name _____   Date of Audit _____

Section 3.5 Production Process

	Standard Clause	Function/Level	Question	Result
228	5.5.1	Shipping associate	Who do you work for? *(Ensure that this matches answer from manager.)*	
229	5.5.3	Shipping associate	How effective is your quality management system? How is this communicated to you?	
230	6.3	Shipping associate	Do you have the equipment and tools you need to do your job?	
231	6.2.2.d	Shipping associate	How do you contribute to the achievement of the quality objectives?	
232	6.2.2.d	Shipping associate	What is the importance of your job?	
233	7.5.3	Shipping associate	What product are you loading and how is it identified?	

Auditor Name _____   Date of Audit _____

Section 3.5 Production Process

	Standard Clause	Function/Level	Question	Result
234	7.6	Shipping associate	For the product that you're loading, what monitoring and measuring devices do you use? *(Record these instruments using Appendix D: Calibration.)*	
235	7.6	Shipping associate	How do you know this measuring device is acceptable to use?	
236	7.5.5	Shipping associate	Does the product that you're loading [name of product: _____] have any requirements for: Handling? Packaging? Storage? Protection? *(Auditor should verify against customer requirements/order/procedures/work instructions.)*	
237	8.2	Shipping associate	For the product that you're loading [name of product: _____], do you monitor and/or measure the product? *(Verify that answer is correct and that measurements were taken at appropriate frequency and met requirements.)*	

Auditor Name _____   Date of Audit _____

Section 3.5 Production Process

	Standard Clause	Function/Level	Question	Result
238	8.3	Shipping associate	What do you do if you find product out of specification? What happens to the product?	
239	8.2.4	Shipping associate	How do you know that the product being loaded is okay to ship?	
240	8.5.2 8.5.3	Shipping associate	Have you participated in any corrective and/or preventive actions? If yes, please give an example.	
241	6.1	Determine by observation in Shipping	*Do resources appear to be adequate to maintain the quality system and continually improve its effectiveness? To enhance customer satisfaction by meeting customer requirements?*	

Auditor Name _____   Date of Audit _____

Section 3.5 Production Process

	Standard Clause	Function/Level	Question	Result
242	6.3	Determine by observation in Shipping	*Infrastructure: Does the area include the appropriate workspace, equipment, and supporting services such as transport or communication?*	
243	6.4	Determine by observation in Shipping	*Is the area's work environment appropriate to meet product requirements?*	
244	4.2.3	All–Shipping	*Randomly sample at least 8 documents in the area to ensure that they meet requirements of document control procedures. Be sure to include the quality manual, procedures, work instructions, forms, and external documents. Use Appendix B: Documents.*	
245	4.2.4	All–Shipping	*Randomly sample at least 4 records in the area to ensure that they meet requirements of record control procedures. Use Appendix C: Records.*	

Auditor Name _____   Date of Audit _____

Section 3.5 Production Process

Use the following section to develop your own questions:

	Procedure/Work Instruction	Function/Level	Question	Result

Auditor Name _____   Date of Audit _____

Section 3.6 Corrective/Preventive Action Process

Interview the person who coordinates the entire corrective and preventive action system. For samples taken, follow up in the areas that were assigned responsibility to verify effectiveness.

	Standard Clause	Question	Result
1	4.2.3 8.5.2	Where is your procedure for corrective action and how is it controlled?	
2	4.2.3 8.5.3	Where is your procedure for preventive action and how is it controlled?	
3	4.2.4 8.5.2	*Sample records of results of action taken for corrective actions utilizing Appendix C: Records.*	
4	4.2.4 8.5.2	*Sample records of results of action taken for preventive actions utilizing Appendix C: Records.*	
5	8.5.2	How do you manage the corrective action process to ensure its effectiveness?	

Auditor Name _____   Date of Audit _____

Section 3.6 Corrective/Preventive Action Process

	Standard Clause	Question	Result
6	4.1.e 8.2.3	How do you measure the effectiveness of the corrective action process?	
7	8.5.1	Can you show me evidence of continual improvement in the corrective and preventive action process?	
8	8.5.2	What internal corrective actions have been issued/assigned to or closed in your plant(s) since the last internal audit? *(Auditor should randomly sample at least 8 corrective actions and ensure that each includes the 5 steps listed below.)* _____ 1 2 3 4 5 6 7 8 1. *Review of the issue* 2. *Identification of the causes* 3. *Evaluation of the need for preventive action* 4. *Determination and implementation of the action needed* 5. *Review of action taken*	

Auditor Name _____   Date of Audit _____

Section 3.6 Corrective/Preventive Action Process

	Standard Clause	Question	Result
9	8.5.2	What customer complaints have been issued/assigned to or closed in your plant(s) since the last internal audit? *(Auditor should randomly sample at least 8 customer complaints and ensure that each includes the 5 steps listed below.)* _____ 1 2 3 4 5 6 7 8 1. *Review of the issue* 2. *Identification of the causes* 3. *Evaluation of the need for preventive action* 4. *Determination and implementation of the action needed* 5. *Review of action taken*	
10	8.5.3	How do you manage the preventive action process to ensure its effectiveness?	
11	4.1.e 8.2.3	How do you measure the effectiveness of the preventive action process?	

Auditor Name _____   Date of Audit _____

Section 3.6 Corrective/Preventive Action Process

	Standard Clause	Question	Result
12	8.5.3	What preventive actions have been issued or closed in your plant(s) since the last internal audit? *(Because this number is usually small, the auditor should review all preventive actions and verify that each includes the 5 steps listed below.)* 1 2 3 4 5 6 7 8 1. *Determination of potential nonconformity* 2. *Identification of its potential causes* 3. *Evaluation of the need for preventive action* 4. *Determination and implementation of the action needed* 5. *Review of action taken*	

Auditor Name _____   Date of Audit _____

Section 3.6 Corrective/Preventive Action Process

Use the following section to develop your own questions:

	Procedure/Work Instruction	Function/Level	Question	Result

Auditor Name _____   Date of Audit _____

Section 3.7 Internal Audit Process

Interview the person who is responsible for the internal audit process. Randomly sample audit records based on the audit plan.

	Standard Clause	Question	Result
1	4.2.3 8.2.2	May I see your procedure for internal quality audits? How is it controlled? *(Auditor to verify that it meets requirements of the standard.)*	
2	4.2.4 8.2.2	*Sample audit results records utilizing Appendix C: Records.*	
3	8.2.2	Please show me your audit plan. *(Auditor to verify that plan meets requirements of standard and procedure. Ensure that audits have been performed to plan.)*	
4	8.2.2	Were audits planned based on the status and importance of the processes to be audited as well as the results of previous audits?	

Auditor Name _____   Date of Audit _____

Section 3.7 Internal Audit Process

	Standard Clause	Question	Result
5	8.2.2	Were the following terms defined: Audit criteria? Scope? Frequency? Methods?	
6	8.2.2 6.2.2	*For each audit sampled, verify that the auditors were trained.*	
7	8.2.2	*For each audit sampled, verify that the auditors did not audit their own work.*	
8	8.2.2	*For nonconformities found, verify that the responsible management ensured actions were taken without undue delay to eliminate problems and their causes.*	

Auditor Name _____   Date of Audit _____

Section 3.7 Internal Audit Process

	Standard Clause	Question	Result
9	8.2.2	*For nonconformities found, ensure that follow-up activities included verification of actions taken and reporting of verification results.*	
10	8.2.2	Did the audit determine that the system met requirements of the standard and company procedure? If so, how? If not, what action will be taken?	
11	8.2.2	Did the audit determine that the system was effectively implemented and maintained? If so, how? If not, what action will be taken?	
12	8.5.1	Show me evidence of continual improvement in the internal audit process.	

Auditor Name _____   Date of Audit _____

Section 3.7 Internal Audit Process

Use the following section to develop your own questions:

Procedure/Work Instruction	Function/Level	Question	Result

Auditor Name _____   Date of Audit _____

Section 3.8 Resource Management/Training Process

	Standard Clause	Function/Level	Question	Result
1	4.1.a	HR manager	What process(es) do you manage?	
2	4.1.b	HR manager	How does your process(es) link with the other processes in the company?	
3	5.1.a	HR manager	How do you communicate to your area the importance of meeting customer, regulatory, and statutory requirements?	
4	5.3.d	HR manager	How do you ensure that the quality policy is communicated and understood?	

Auditor Name _____   Date of Audit _____

Section 3.8 Resource Management/Training Process

	Standard Clause	Function/Level	Question	Result
5	5.4.1	HR manager	What are the quality objectives for your area?	
6	5.4.2	HR manager	How do you ensure that the integrity of the quality management system is maintained when changes are planned and implemented?	
7	5.5.1	HR manager	Where are responsibilities and authorities defined for the plant including HR, and how are they communicated?	
8	5.5.3	HR manager	What communication processes are established within your area?	

Auditor Name _____   Date of Audit _____

Section 3.8 Resource Management/Training Process

	Standard Clause	Function/Level	Question	Result
9	5.5.3	HR manager	How do you communicate the effectiveness of the quality management system to your area?	
10	6.1.a	HR manager	How does the company determine and provide the resources needed to maintain and continually improve the effectiveness of the quality system?	
11	6.1.b	HR manager	How does the company determine and provide the resources needed to improve customer satisfaction by meeting their requirements?	
12	6.2.1	HR manager	How do you determine competence of your employees? *Salaried:* *Hourly:*	

Auditor Name _____   Date of Audit _____

Section 3.8 Resource Management/Training Process

	Standard Clause	Function/Level	Question	Result
13	6.2.2.c	HR manager	How do you evaluate training effectiveness? Please show examples as evidence.	
14	6.2.2.d	HR manager	How do you ensure that personnel in HR are aware of the importance of their jobs and how they contribute to achievement of quality objectives?	
15	8.2.3	HR manager	What do you do when planned results are not achieved? *(Response should provide examples of correction and corrective action.)*	

Auditor Name _____   Date of Audit _____

Section 3.8 Resource Management/Training Process

	Standard Clause	Function/Level	Question	Result
16	8.2.3 4.1.e	HR manager	How do you monitor and measure your process? Please provide examples. *(Response should include data pertaining to characteristics and trends of process.)*	
17	8.4	HR manager	What data does your area collect and analyze pertaining to opportunities for preventive actions?	
18	8.5.1	HR manager	Please provide examples of continual improvement in your area(s) of responsibility.	
19	8.5.2	HR manager	What internal corrective actions have been issued/assigned to or closed in your area(s) since the last internal audit? *(Auditor should randomly sample at least 6 corrective actions.)*	

Auditor Name _____   Date of Audit _____

Section 3.8 Resource Management/Training Process

	Standard Clause	Function/Level	Question	Result
20	8.5.3	HR manager	What preventive actions have been issued or closed in your area(s) since the last internal audit? *(Because this number is usually small, the auditor should review all preventive actions.)*	
21	5.1.a	Training coordinator	How does the company communicate the importance of meeting customer, regulatory, and statutory requirements to you?	
22	5.3.d	Training coordinator	What does the quality policy mean to you?	
23	5.4.1	Training coordinator	What are the quality objectives for your area?	

Auditor Name _____   Date of Audit _____

Section 3.8 Resource Management/Training Process

	Standard Clause	Function/Level	Question	Result
24	5.5.1	Training coordinator	What are your primary responsibilities? *(If not documented, ensure that this matches answer from manager.)*	
25	5.5.1	Training coordinator	Who do you work for? *(Ensure that this matches answer from manager.)*	
26	5.5.3	Training coordinator	How effective is your quality management system? How is this communicated to you?	
27	6.3	Training coordinator	Do you have the equipment and tools you need to do your job?	
28	6.2.2.d	Training coordinator	How do you contribute to the achievement of the quality objectives?	

Auditor Name _____   Date of Audit _____

Section 3.8 Resource Management/Training Process

	Standard Clause	Function/Level	Question	Result
29	6.2.2.d	Training coordinator	What is the importance of your job?	
30	8.5.2 8.5.3	Training coordinator	Have you participated in any corrective and/or preventive actions? If yes, please give an example.	
31	6.2.2	Training coordinator	*Randomly sample employees interviewed, using Appendix F: Interview Sheet. Be certain to sample employees from each process and level in the organization. Ensure that each employee has a record indicating competence to do the job he or she was performing while interviewed. Check off each employee sampled for training in the third column of Appendix F: Interview Sheet. In the fourth column, indicate whether competency and training requirements were met. Don't forget to include the plant manager.*	

Auditor Name _____   Date of Audit _____

Section 3.8 Resource Management/Training Process

Use the following section to develop your own questions:

Procedure/Work Instruction	Function/Level	Question	Result

Auditor Name _____   Date of Audit _____

Section 3.9 Product Realization Process

To ensure that the entire product realization process is working, randomly choose a product that shipped sometime during the previous month.

Product: _____   Customer: _____

Date of production: _____   Date of shipment: _____   Carrier: _____

	Clause	Instructions for Auditor	OK?
1	7.1 7.3	Check the records for planning of product realization and design.	
2	7.2	Obtain the record of the order and any customer-specific requirements. Ensure that the order was processed properly. Verify that all customer-specific requirements were met throughout the rest of this audit.	

Auditor Name _____   Date of Audit _____

Section 3.9 Product Realization Process

	Clause	Instructions for Auditor	OK?
3	7.5.3	Verify that the order is traceable back to the raw materials. List all raw materials.	
4	7.4	Check records of these raw materials to ensure that they were received and inspected as required. Sample any measuring devices that were used on *Appendix D*: Calibration.	
5	7.4	Verify that the suppliers of the raw materials and the carrier were approved and had been evaluated and reevaluated.	
6	7.4	Verify the purchase orders for the raw materials and carrier.	

Auditor Name _____   Date of Audit _____

Section 3.9 Product Realization Process

	Clause	Instructions for Auditor	OK?
7	7.5	Verify production records to ensure that process parameters were met.	
8	8.2.4	Verify in-process and final inspection records to ensure that all tests and inspections were performed and met requirements.	

Auditor Name _____   Date of Audit _____

Conclusion

Your process approach audit checklist will only improve with time as you add more and more questions specific to your organization. I suggest that your organization collect questions from different auditors across different processes to optimize the checklist. And keep in mind that the checklist should be a living document—changing and growing with your organization and its auditors.

Auditing is not for everyone, but proper training and the right tools make it much more effective, enjoyable, and easier for those who audit only occasionally. It is my sincerest hope that this manual has left you better prepared as both an auditor and an auditee. When I took my first auditing class 10 years ago, I never dreamed I would be a professional auditor today. Who knows? It might happen to you.

HAPPY AUDITING!

Appendix A
Purchasing

Raw Material	Material Code	Lot Number	Supplier	Date Rec'd	Proper ID?	Inspection Completed & Material Passed?	C of A Avail if Req'd?	Approved Supplier?	Supplier Selected Properly?	Supplier Evaluated?	Supplier Reevaluated?	PO Adequate and Includes QMS Requirements?	Adequacy Confirmed Prior to Order?
1													
2													
3													
4													
5													
6													
7													
8													
9													
10													
11													
12													
Provider of Calibration Services													
1	X	X		X	X	X	X						
2	X	X		X	X	X	X						
3	X	X		X	X	X	X						
Carriers													
1	X	X		X	X	X	X						
2	X	X		X	X	X	X						
3	X	X		X	X	X	X						
Other Service Providers													
1	X	X		X	X	X	X						
2	X	X		X	X	X	X						

Appendix B
Documents

Name	Doc #	Rev #/Date	Location	Master List Rev #/Date	Review & Approval	OK?
1						
2						
3						
4						
5						
6						
7						
8						
9						
10						
11						
12						
13						
14						
15						
16						
17						
18						
19						
20						
21						
22						
23						

Appendix C
Records

Name	Location	Legible?	Retrievable?	Protected?	Retention Time Required	Actual Time Retained	Disposition?
1							
2							
3							
4							
5							
6							
7							
8							
9							
10							
11							
12							
13							
14							
15							
16							
17							
18							
19							
20							
21							

Appendix D
Calibration

Type of Instrument	ID Number	Location	Last Calibrated	Calibration Due Date	Calibration Interval Established	In Tolerance?	Traceable Standard Used?
1							
2							
3							
4							
5							
6							
7							
8							
9							
10							
11							
12							
13							
14							
15							
16							
17							
18							
19							
20							
21							

Appendix E
Management Review

Date of Meeting: _____

Did REVIEW INPUT include: **(yes or no for each)**

1. Audit results?	
2. Customer feedback?	
3. Process performance?	
4. Product conformity?	
5. Status of corrective actions?	
6. Status of preventive actions?	
7. Follow-up actions from previous management reviews?	
8. Changes that could affect the quality system including the quality policy and quality objectives?	
9. Recommendations for improvement?	

**Did REVIEW OUTPUT include decisions
and actions related to:**   **(yes or no for each)**

1. Improvement of the system's effectiveness and its processes?	
2. Improvement of the product in relation to customer requirements?	
3. Resource needs?	

Other   **(yes or no for each)**

Were all areas represented at the meeting?	
Was the review conducted within the established time frame?	
Were records maintained as required?	
Was the system found suitable, adequate, and effective?	
Was the policy reviewed for continuing suitability?	

Appendix F
Interview Sheet

The following persons were interviewed and provided evidence:

Print Name	Print Department and Title Auditor should verify that title matches job being done during the audit	Competency	Policy/ Objective?

Appendix G
Management Review
Meeting Checklist

Date of Meeting: _____

Meeting Attendee	Title
_____	_____
_____	_____
_____	_____
_____	_____
_____	_____

Use a separate sheet if necessary

REVIEW INPUT

1. Audit results:
2. Customer feedback:
3. Process performance:
4. Product conformity:
5. Status of corrective actions:
6. Status of preventive actions:
7. Follow-up actions from previous management reviews:
8. Changes that could affect the quality system including quality policy/objectives:
9. Recommendations for improvement:
10. Summary of supplier performance:

REVIEW OUTPUT

1. Improvement of the system's effectiveness and its processes:
2. Improvement of the product in relation to customer requirements:
3. Resource needs:

Was the system found suitable, adequate, and effective?	
Does the policy continue to be suitable? If no, what changes should be made?	

References

1. ISO/TC 176/SC 1/N 215, ISO/TC 176/SC 2/N 526R, *ISO 9000 Introduction and Support Package: Guidance on Terminology Used in ISO 9001:2000 and ISO 9004:2000,* p. 6.
2. ANSI/ISO/ASQ Q9000-2000, *Quality management systems—Fundamentals and vocabulary,* ASQ Quality Press, 2000, section 3.9.12.
3. ANSI/ISO/ASQ Q9000-2000, *Quality management systems—Fundamentals and vocabulary,* ASQ Quality Press, 2000, section 3.9.3.
4. ANSI/ISO/ASQ Q9001-2000, *American National Standard Quality management systems—Requirements,* ASQ Quality Press, 2000.

Index